Gemäldegalerie Berlin

Old Master Paintings

Prestel

Munich · London · New York

© Prestel Verlag
Munich · London · New York, and Staatliche Museen zu Berlin – Stiftung Preußischer Kulturbesitz, 1998, 6th edition, 2014

© for plans shown on the inside covers by the Gemäldegalerie der Staatlichen Museen zu Berlin

© for illustrated works by the Staatliche Museen zu Berlin Preussischer Kulturbesitz (The plans were based on data supplied by Ingenieurbüro Volker Doose, Berlin)

Photos: Jörg P. Anders, Volker H. Schneider, Christoph Schmidt, Gemäldegalerie der Staatlichen Museen zu Berlin

Editor: Rainald Grosshans (1st to 3rd editions), Rainer Michaelis (4th and 5th editions)

Translated from the German by Michael Robinson, London
Copy-edited by Jane Milosch, Munich
5th edition: translation and copy-editing by John Sykes, Cologne

Front cover:
Frans Hals, Catharina Hooft with her Nurse (detail), c. 1619/20 (see no. 127)

Back cover:
Staatliche Museen zu Berlin – Gemäldegalerie; Photo: Jörg P. Anders

Prestel Verlag, Munich
A member of Verlagsgruppe Random House GmbH
Neumarkter Strasse 28
81673 Munich
Tel. +49 (0)89 4136-0
Fax +49 (0)89 4136-2335
www.prestel.de

Prestel Publishing Ltd.
14-17 Wells Street
London W1T 3PD
Tel. +44 (0)20 7323-5004
Fax +44 (0)20 7323-0271

Prestel Publishing
900 Broadway, Suite 603
New York, NY 10003 USA
Tel. +1 (212) 995-2720
Fax +1(212) 995-2733
www.prestel.com

Prestel books are available worldwide. Please contact your nearest bookseller or write to one of the above addresses for information concerning your local distributor.

Printed in Germany on acid-free paper
ISBN 978-3-7913-5207-7 (English edition)
ISBN 978-3-7913-5206-0 (German edition)

Designed by Maja Kluy, Berlin
Cover designed by: SOFAROBOTNIK, Augsburg & Munich
Type set by ew print & medien service gmbh, Würzburg
Lithography by Fotolito Longo, Frangart
Printed and bound by Aumüller Druck Regensburg

Gemäldegalerie
Staatliche Museen zu Berlin
Preussischer Kulturbesitz
Kulturforum, Berlin-Tiergarten
Matthäikirchplatz
Management: Stauffenbergstrasse 40
10785 Berlin
Tel.: +49 (0)30 266 42 40 01
Fax: +49 (0)30 266 40 10

www.smb.museum

Opening hours
Tuesday–Sunday: 10 a.m. to 6 p.m.
Thursday: 10 a.m. to 8 p.m.
Closed on Mondays

Staatliche Museen info line
Tel.: +49 (0)30 266 42 30 40

Guided tours
Reservations for school groups and other groups:
Tel.: +49 (0)30 266 42 42 42
service@smb.museum

Guided tours on specialist themes
Thursdays and Saturdays: 2.30 p.m.

Guided tour of museum
Sundays: 2.30 p.m.

Appraisals
Telephone reservations required

Frequent visitors to the Gemäldegalerie enjoy many advantages by becoming a member of the **Kaiser Friedrich-Museums-Verein**, the painting and sculpture galleries' supporters association. For further information, please contact the secretary of the Kaiser Friedrich-Museums-Verein
Tuesday/Wednesday: 10 a.m. to 3 p.m.
Tel. +49 (0)30 266 42 40 02
Fax +49 (0)30 266 40 10

Verlagsgruppe Random House FSC® N001967
The FSC®-certified paper *Galaxi Keramik* was supplied by Papier-Union, Ehingen

FSC
www.fsc.org
MIX
Paper from responsible sources
FSC® C017373

Contents

Introduction

History of the Gemäldegalerie

In 1998 the Berlin Gemäldegalerie opened a new building at the Kulturforum. The paintings which had survived the war only to be seen separated from each other in the east and west sectors of the city—in the Bode-Museum and the Dahlem Museum—could now be united and shown together. Its treasures restored, the Gemäldegalerie once again houses one of the world's greatest collections of paintings. A rich repository of celebrated masterpieces, it overwhelms visitors with a lavishly comprehensive survey of European painting from the 13th to the close of the 18th century.

There are larger and even perhaps more important collections of paintings. Yet no other was conceived from the beginning on such stringently didactic principles. In 1797 the archaeologist Aloys Hirt (1759–1839) had proposed the foundation of a public museum of European art. Its collections were to be organised on strictly scholarly principles. Hirt's insistence on strict adherence to Enlightenment ideals was modified by leading members of a younger generation, among them the architect Karl Friedrich Schinkel (1781–1841) and the scholarly connoisseur Carl Friedrich von Ruhmor (1785–1848). Like other exponents of the Romantic notion of art, they expected art to "give pleasure first and then instruct".

The new approach to art soon prevailed. Pictures embodying the Romantic ideal were selected and preparations for the new museum began. Schinkel not only drew the plans for it; he also proposed its site: the section of the Lustgarten across from the Royal Palace façade designed by Schlüter. That this still vacant site could be considered at all, indeed that it was approved by the royal patron, King Friedrich Wilhelm III, is a clear indication of the status that would be accorded to Berlin's first public museum.

As architecture, too, the structure was notable. Built on a rectangular plan, it had two storeys. Despite the building's austere simplicity of form, the façade facing the Lustgarten is dominated by a grand, full-length colonnade counterbalancing the central domed interior space. When the building, now known as the Altes Museum, was inaugurated in 1830, the antiquities collection was housed on the ground floor. The paintings were hung on the upper floor. This

Karl Friedrich Schinkel, Altes Museum, 1823–30

gallery was a remarkable achievement. Its strengths were both aesthetic and didactic. The works exhibited were definitive masterpieces. Moreover, they had been selected stylistically as being representative of both periods and schools.

Unlike the earlier great dynastic collections—in Florence, Vienna, Paris, Madrid, Munich or Dresden—the Berlin collections did not centre on the High Renaissance and the Baroque. For the first time, the so-called Primitives, late medieval and Early Renaissance masters, were represented. In this connection it should be mentioned that the provenance of most of the near 1200 paintings which formed the nucleus of the inaugural collection did not come from Hohenzollern palaces. On the contrary, purchase of these works did not begin until 1815.

That year, a few months after the victory at Waterloo, the Prussian government bought the Marchese Vincenzo Giustiniani (1564–1637) collection in Paris. It did not match the prevailing Neo-Classical taste but brought early Italian Baroque, the realism of Caravaggio and his followers, to the museum. Other works were selectively acquired.

The Gallery owes its reputation to the collection owned by the English merchant Edward Solly (1776–1848), purchased in 1821 with private royal funds. Hirt, Schinkel and Gustav Friedrich Waagen (1794–1848), a pupil of Ruhmor's, had the difficult task of critically evaluating this inventory of 3000 paintings, ultimately selecting 677 works for the museum.

Solly's main interest as a collector had been in Italian painting, not merely the classic masters (Raphael, Titian, Paris Bordon, Lorenzo Lotto, Savoldo) but also their predecessors. The Gallery owes its outstanding collection of Quattrocento (Filippo Lippi, Castagno, Pollaiuollo, Botticelli, Mantegna, Carpaccio, Bellini, Cima) and Trecento paintings (Giotto, Taddeo Gaddi, Bernardo Daddi,

Wilhelm Hensel, Karl Friedrich Schinkel; Staatliche Museen zu Berlin, Nationalgalerie

Alegretto Nuzi, Lippo Memmi, Pietro Lorenzetti) to Solly's passion for collecting and his profound knowledge of art. It endowed the museum with major works of Early Netherlandish painting, among them the six panels, painted on both sides, of the van Eyck brothers' Ghent Altar. The Solly Collection also contained masterpieces of early German painting like the altarpiece panels

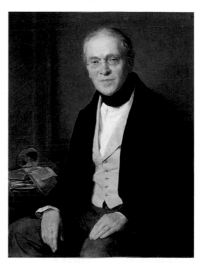

Ludwig Knaus, Gustav Friedrich Waagen; Staatliche Museen zu Berlin, Nationalgalerie

Ernst Eberhard von Ihne, The Kaiser Friedrich-Museum, 1898–1904

executed by the Master of the Darmstadt Passion and Hans Holbein the Younger's portrait *The Merchant Georg Gisze* (no. 45). The importance of the Solly Collection in enhancing the museum's reputation cannot, even now, be underestimated.

A few months after the museum's inauguration, Wilhelm von Humboldt, the Prussian minister charged with supervising the building of the museum, wrote to the king:

> "Many galleries, perhaps all the known ones, can only be regarded as aggregates which have gradually emerged without any underlying plan. The Royal Gallery here, on the other hand, is notable for systematically encompassing all periods of painting."

Gustav Friedrich Waagen was appointed as the Gallery's first director. Although the exhilarating idealism of the early years had ebbed so that funds were no longer generously forthcoming, about 345 paintings were acquired during his tenure (1830–68). Among them were Titian's *Girl with Dish of Fruit*, three Rogier van der Weyden altarpieces (The Virgin, the Middelburg and the St. John Altars, nos. 55, 56, 58), Gossaert's night-piece with *Christ on the Mount of Olives* (no. 84), van Dyck's *Portrait of Carignan* and Cornelis de Vos's enchanting double portrait of the artist's children (no. 113). Waagen also succeeded in enlarging the museum's collection of panel paintings. With the purchase of the collection owned by the Berlin publisher Reimer (1843), a number of major genre pieces were added to the 17th-century Dutch paintings.

Disagreement on acquisitions policy with the Deputy Director Ignatz von Olferts, appointed in 1839, and exponents of archaeology advocating a plaster-cast collection of Classical Greco-Roman sculpture, greatly impeded Waagen's further efforts for the museum. He only managed to acquire a few more pieces. Among them, however, were such matchless works as Raphael's *Madonna Terranuova* (no. 195), a tondo dating from the master's Florentine period, and the two Stauffer retables acquired in 1862 from the Wiesenkirche Church at Soest.

The Gallery is indebted to Wilhelm von Bode (1845–1929), who began his museum career in 1872, for his auspicious acquisitions in all areas and the museum's advancement to world-class status. Like Waagen, he was exceptionally knowledgeable about art and a talented organiser. Sound understanding and inexhaustible energy enabled him to turn the sweeping changes taking place in his day to advantage in pursuing his goals.

After the foundation of the German Empire in 1871, which elevated Berlin to the status of an imperial capital, the Gallery and the other divisions of the Royal Museums were expected to represent the nation's grandeur. The new power united in Prussia after the victory over France was matched by a general economic upturn. Generous museum funding was now available.

In 1874 the largest German private collection of its day was acquired from the industrialist Barthold Suermondt. It included two Hans Holbein the Younger portraits and major Early Netherlandish paintings, among them Jan van Eyck's *The Madonna in the Church* (no. 49). The focus of the collection was on Dutch painting. Five paintings by Frans Hals, a "sampling" of ter Borch, Jan Steen, Jan Vermeer and numerous other masters were now in public possession.

It was characteristic of Bode that he attached equal importance to acquisitions policy and scholarship. His preoccupation

Max Liebermann, Wilhelm von Bode, pastel; Staatliche Museen zu Berlin, Gemäldegalerie

with Rembrandt's work endowed the Gallery with a rich treasure trove of acquisitions ranging from *The Parable of the Rich Man* (1627), the monumental portrait of *The Mennonite Preacher Anslo and His Wife* (1641, no. 140) to the sumptuous late works like *Joseph and Potiphar's Wife* (1655, no. 142) and the *Portrait of Hendrickje Stoffels (Young Woman at the Open Door)*, (c. 1659, no. 143).

Bode's acquisitions policy was not confined to enlarging the Gallery's inventory of Dutch painting. He also bought important works by Rubens and other Flemish masters. He collaborated with Max J. Friedländer to enlarge the collection of Early Netherlandish paintings, making it undeniably the best of its kind. He also left Italian painting, especially the Early Renaissance masters, superbly represented.

With its collections growing by leaps and bounds, Schinkel's Altes Museum was no longer large enough to house them. However, it would be some time before a new building was erected to house the paintings and works of religious art—the sculpture collection.

In 1904, a museum built to plans by Ernst von Ihnes entirely in the

Wilhelmine style was inaugurated on the northern tip of the Museumsinsel. Though christened as the Kaiser Friedrich Museum after the patron of Prussian museums, Emperor Friedrich III, the museum was actually Bode's creation. From 1890, as Director of the Gallery and Sculpture Collection, he was able to realise his plans for uniting the various genres and media in an integrated presentation of painting, sculpture and art objects in the new museum.

The Kaiser Friedrich-Museums-Verein (Museum Association) also owes its foundation to his commitment. Its acquisitions policy gave the most effective support to his systematic enlargement of the collections.

By the outbreak of the First World War, the new museum's collections had become so large that once again more space was needed.

Bode did not live to see the Deutsches Museum inaugurated in 1930 in the north wing of the Pergamon Museum designed by Alfred Messel.

The Second World War, even more than the First World War, and its consequences interrupted the steady growth of the Gallery. The works of art it contained had to be protected from bombing raids. Some were put into Thuringian salt mines for safe keeping. Others, including major paintings in large formats, remained in Berlin. When the city surrendered on 2 May, 1945, there were still 434 undamaged paintings in the Friedrichshain Flak Bunker, an air-raid shelter within the city limits. Not long after Soviet troops had taken it over, fire broke out which—as had always been feared—destroyed the paintings. This catastrophe, and the partitioning of the city, seemingly marked the end of the renowned collections. However, in both the east and west sectors of the city, persistent efforts were being made to keep reconstruction work going.

General Dwight D. Eisenhower (centre) visits the paintings stored in the Kaiseroda mine

Bruno Paul, the Museum Dahlem, 1913–16

The paintings stored in the salt mines—numbering 1225 in total—were rescued by American troops and brought to a storehouse in Wiesbaden. In 1950 the first exhibition, comprised of 149 paintings, was sent to Berlin from Wiesbaden. However, the state of Hesse insisted on the pictures being returned. Not until 1955, when the Kaiser Friedrich-Museums-Verein successfully sued for the return of the paintings belonging to it, did the state governments of the western federal states agree to return to (West) Berlin the art treasures which had once belonged to Prussia. In 1957 the German Bundestag enacted legislation providing for the foundation of the Stiftung Preussischer Kulturbesitz (Endowment for Prussian Cultural Possessions). By this time all the paintings had been returned to be hung in the Dahlem Museum.

The Dahlem Museum building, designed by Bruno Paul, was originally erected for a different purpose. Intended to relieve congestion on the Museumsinsel by housing Asian art, the Asiatisches Museum had been used from 1923 as a magazine for the ethnological collections. In view of the destruction of the city, it was indeed fortunate that the works of art could be housed at all in the Dahlem Museum. Yet, due to unfavourable light conditions and lack of space, this building had always been regarded as a stopgap measure. Consequently, there had been talk of rebuilding the Gallery on the southern fringe of the Tiergarten since the early 1960s.

The roughly 1000 pictures which survived the war in the Museumsinsel air-raid shelters faced problems of a different magnitude. After makeshift repairs to remedy the worst bomb damage, an exhibition of a few paintings was inaugurated as early as 1953 in the Museum am Kupfergraben, then known as the Kaiser Friedrich Museum (since 1956 the Bode-Museum).

By the time works of art had been returned from the former Soviet Union in 1958, among them the sculpture from the Pergamon Altar, rooms had been made available to house paintings and sculpture in the north wing of the museum of that same name (formerly the Deutsches Museum). After museum operations had returned to normal, acquisitions once again resumed.

Heinz Hilmer and Christoph Sattler, elevation of the new Gemäldegalerie, 1992–98

Under the directorship of Irene Geismeier, the focus was on purchasing 17th-century Dutch masters for the Bode-Museum. This policy resulted in a shift in emphasis with regard to the surviving inventory. More generously available funding and links with the international art market made buying art easier in the western part of the city. From the outset, purchases of single works went well.

Focused collecting did not start until later. Under the directorship of Robert Oertel (1964–72), the collection of Italian Baroque paintings was systematically enlarged. His successor, Henning Bock, succeeded in having a new section on 18th-century English painting added to the traditional divisions of the Gallery. Henning Bock was also in charge of ensuring that the division he headed was restructured and expertly staffed in compliance with an administrative measure in force from 1 January, 1992, unifying Berlin's municipal museums. Further, he played a major role in the planning of the building, which was almost finished by the end of his tenure (1973–96).

The new Gemäldegalerie was designed by the architects Heinz Hilmer and Christoph Sattler. Its exterior is restrained in style, enclosing the Kulturforum at the corner of Sigismund and Stauffenberg Streets within a block-like structure. Superbly adapted to the urban-planning conditions imposed by its setting, the new Gemäldegalerie was conceived as a whole with the museum and other cultural buildings already on the site. Still it has its own distinctive "look". The façades, dressed with closely fitted terracotta panels above a high rusticated plinth, are clearly articulated. Even the colour signifies that this is architecture reminiscent of both the Florentine Renaissance and Prussian Neo-Classicism. The outer shell of the building, recalling an austerely mounted reliquary, signals that its contents are precious.

Its interior also underscores the stature of the Berlin painting collections. It incorporates a central hall subdivided by two rows of piers. The flat vaulting of this part of the building is surmounted by domes of clear glass allowing daylight to shine in unrefracted. The varying intensity of sunlight lends character to the interior space, but prohibits the installation of paintings.

The new Gemäldegalerie, the large hall with the 5–7–9 Series by Walter de Maria

The hall has been conceived as a place for contemplation, a function suggested by an artwork entitled *5–7–9 Series*, installed in a shallow basin of water—a series of polygonal, highly polished stainless steel rods by the American Conceptual artist Walter de Maria. The exhibition rooms lead around the hall in a double U-shape, articulated outwardly to form rooms and cabinets. Even the exhibition rooms receive daylight from above. However, it does not penetrate into them directly but is filtered to spread uniform lightness. Distracting reflections have been eschewed. Embellishment enough has been provided by a floor of smoky dark oak and a velvet wall covering that absorbs light. The end result is that the paintings themselves appear to "ignite" via the diffused light so that colour is given its full hue, value and saturation.

Arranged around both sides and at the main end of the hall, the exhibition rooms imply a topographical and chronological ordering of European art in schools south and north of the Alps. At the end, a linking tract forms a transverse axis where the 17th and 18th-century Dutch, French and English paintings have been installed. In all there are 53 exhibition rooms with a hanging surface 1800 metres long on which about 850 paintings have been placed. The ground-floor study/educational galleries house 400 more paintings.

Let there be no mistake: the division into main and study galleries does not imply a division in the inventory. The notion that the best of the Berlin Gallery was exhibited in the Dahlem Museum, whereas what was left was on view in the Bode Museum, is only partly true. On the Museumsinsel paintings of outstanding stature have survived, among them works which, because of their monumental size, could not be stored for safe keeping during the war.

A judgement about which part of the various collections have come together neatly and which have not, will not be necessary. What has been assembled in the new building from the Dahlem "refuge" and the Bode-Museum is a collection that grew as a seamless entity and now has once again assumed its original diversity and distinction.

Knowledge of art is something which grows with us. Therefore, it is a quality which is always being redefined as long as the spectator is willing to be open to

The new Gemäldegalerie, the Caravaggio Room

art. A museum's task is to awaken this readiness by promoting personal encounters with works of art, and this is equally true of museum publication policy.

Jan Kelch
Director of the Gemäldegalerie
(1996–2004)

Since the reopening of the Bode-Museum in autumn 2006, the Gemäldegalerie has exhibited works from its collection there too. The paintings have been chosen in order to display under one roof, in collaboration with the Sculpture Collection, works made using both artistic techniques, where possible in direct proximity.

Bernd W. Lindemann.
Director of the Gemäldegalerie

Principal Works in the Collection

13th to 18th-Century Painting

The Authors

Claudia Banz	CB	Bernd Lindemann	BL
Roberto Contini	RC	Rainer Michaelis	RM
Irene Geismeier	IG	Stefan Moret	SM
Rainald Grosshans †	RG	Hannelore Nützmann	HN
Kathrin Höltge	KH	Matthias Weniger	MW
Stephan Kemperdick	SK		

Westphalian, c. 1230/40

1   Crucifixion Altarpiece from Soest
Parchment on oak, 86 x 195.5 cm
Acquired 1862

This altarpiece is one of the earliest of
its kind to survive in Germany. Mary,
the other women and John are standing
below the cross in the centre, and next to
them are the Roman captain and staring people. Personifications of Ecclesia
and Synagogue appear on galleries at
the sides of the cross. In the left-hand
panel Christ is being presented to the
High Priest Caiaphas, who addresses
him with the banderole "How long dost
thou make us to doubt? If thou be the
Christ, tell us plainly." The right-hand
panel shows Mary and her companions
at the tomb. An angel is sitting on the
sarcophagus, pointing to the empty tomb
and proclaiming Christ's resurrection

from the dead. The ornamental strips in
relief and sunken pictorial fields imitate
gold work. Hard, crystalline ridged folds
are juxtaposed with rounded drapery.
These are characteristic of a stylistic
development known as the "Zackenstil"
(jagged, serrated style).   *RG*

Westphalian, after 1250

2   Altarpiece with the Throne of Mercy
Oak, 71 x 120 cm
Acquired 1862

The arches and pilasters have survived
from the original frame of the altarpiece
and divide the picture into three fields of
equal size.
    The central field shows the Holy
Trinity with God the Father on the
throne, Christ on the cross and the Holy
Spirit in the form of a dove. God the

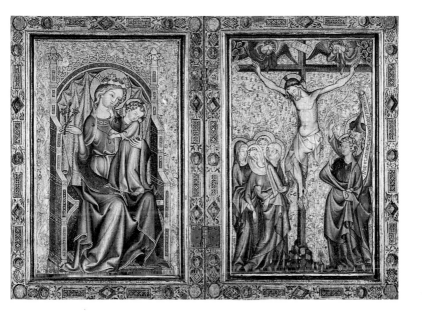

Father is identified as the beginning and the end by the alpha and omega which are to be seen by his head. He is showing the viewer his dead son on the cross, which seems to grow out of a rock. This is a vivid representation of the dual nature of Christ, who is both God and man.

This representation of the Trinity symbolises the sacrifice of the Son of God, while revealing the grace of God the Father. It also refers to the repetition of the same sacrifice witnessed in the mass. On the left and right are Mary and John, who have come to God's throne to intercede for grace for sinful mankind.

The rest of the architectural frame, the gold ground and the glowing colours are reminiscent of reliquaries or retables in gold and coloured enamel. The characteristic feature of the design is the geometrical and crystalline stylisation in the arrangement of the drapery. The exaggeration and abstraction of the stylistic elements are typical of the late phase of the so-called "Zackenstil" (jagged, serrated style), seen here at its most mature.   *RG*

Cologne, c. 1300

3   Cologne Diptych
Oak, each panel 19.5 x 34 cm
Acquired in 1902 by Sir Charles Robinson, London

The diptych is one of very few surviving panel paintings in the High Gothic style, of which it is an example of the very highest quality. The left-hand wing shows Mary with the child, enthroned as the Queen of Heaven. In her right hand she holds a rose branch, a symbol associated with Mary. The rose without thorns was a reference to the bride of the Song of Solomon, who like Mary was without sin. The right-hand wing shows Christ on the cross, mourned by two hovering angels. Under the cross on the left are Mary and her companions, on the right John and the prophet Isaiah with a banderole bearing a Latin inscription meaning: "He has been wounded for our transgressions." This Old Testament text was always interpreted as a prophecy of the sacrifice on the cross, which had now been consummated. The work is in an unusually good state of preservation and still possesses the original frame with its imitation enamel-work and fittings.   *RG*

Bohemian, c. 1350

5 The Crucifixion of Christ
(Kaufmann Crucifixion)
Canvas on wood, 67.7 x 30.3 cm
Acquired 1918

The cross of Christ is in the centre,
with the thieves' crosses on either side.
Beneath the cross is the Roman captain
Longinus, piercing Christ's side with his
lance. Opposite him is the good captain,
testifying that Christ truly is the Son
of God. On the left are John and Mary
with her companions. Mary Magdalene
is desperately embracing the stem of
the cross. On the right at the front the
executioner's henchmen are throwing dice for Christ's robe. The lavish
detail, refined painterly composition
and powerful presentation lend tangible
expression to the drama of this
event.   RG

Bohemian, c. 1340/50

4 Mary Enthroned with the Child
(Glatz Madonna)
Poplar, 186 x 95 cm
Acquired in 1902 through the
Kaiser Friedrich-Museums-Verein.
Accession to this museum in 1905.

Mary is sitting with the child on an
ornate throne. The lily-sceptre and the
orb identify her as the Queen of Heaven,
and two lions in the body of the throne
allude to the throne of Solomon. In the
Middle Ages Mary was perceived as the
seat of wisdom, with Christ enthroned
on her lap as the new Solomon. The
donor Ernst von Pardubitz (d. 1364), the
first Archbishop of Prague, is kneeling at
Mary's feet. He was appointed bishop in
1343, after studying in Italy and Paris.
He raised Prague to the status of archbishopric in 1344, making the city
independent from the archbishopric of
Mainz.   RG

Westphalian, c. 1420/30

**6 The Holy Face of Christ
(Vera Icon)**
Oak, with frame 49.5 x 35 cm
Acquired 1843

The picture shows Christ's face, frontally and perfectly symmetrical, with his eyes fixed on the viewer. The head with long, parted hair and divided beard is surrounded by a golden mandorla with a Latin inscription running round it. It means: "I am the beginning and the end – God and Man". According to legend, the true likeness of Christ was handed down either through an imprint of his face on a piece of cloth, or from a painting by the Apostle Luke. The most widespread legend was that St. Veronica handed Christ her veil on his way to the crucifixion, and that his face was imprinted on it. There is a series of images of Christ that are particularly venerated as relics because they are believed to have been created during his lifetime. The representation of Christ's face, usually on St. Veronica's veil, was used for the worship of the Divine Countenance, a cult that gained significance from the 13th century.   *RG*

Austrian, c. 1420

**7 Christ as Man of Sorrows with
St. John and the Virgin**
Fir wood, with frame 25.5 x 34 cm
Acquired in 1918

This small panel, one of the most poetic works of the so-called International Style, depicts an obviously unique scene that is closely linked to the events of the Passion of Christ, yet has been separated from them: evening has fallen at the place of crucifixion, and the last executioner is hurrying home to Jerusalem on the right through the city gate. In the complete silence that has descended on Golgotha, Mary and Christ's favourite disciple John are mourning him. Christ has been removed from the cross, but is not lying on the knees of his mother as a corpse as usual, but sitting against the upright of the cross as the Man of Sorrows. In this way Christ represents mortal man and at the same time immortal God. Accordingly he is not depicted as deceased; rather his posture expresses the pains and exhaustion that he has taken upon himself for the salvation of mankind. A melancholy mood weighs upon the scene, and the two mourners seem to be more sunk in meditation than paralysed by grief. On the left next to Christ can be seen the sarcophagus that has been prepared for him in a rock tomb and from which he will arise after three days, and several instruments of his Passion: the nails, the loincloth, the lance and the sponge with vinegar.   *SK*

This altar, which gave the anonymous master his name, was commissioned by Nuremberg patrician Berthold Deichsler (d. 1418/19) and his second wife, Katherina Zenner (d. 1438) for the Behaim Chapel in the Nuremberg Dominican monastery church. The altar wings that have survived could originally be opened out; their front and back sections were later separated. The outer sides of the wings show Mary with the child and St. Peter. When open, the shrine was flanked on the inside of the wings by SS. Elizabeth of Thuringia and John the Baptist, standing under Gothic baldacchinos on low plinths against a golden background. The elegance of the lines and lavish play of undulating folds in the garments are reminiscent of late Bohemian painting. RG

Master of the Older Holy Kindred Altarpiece
(1st third of the 15th century)

9   Mary Triptych, c. 1410/20
Oak, in the original frames,
central panel 40 x 35.5 cm,
each wing 40 x 17.5 cm
Acquired with the Solly Collection, 1821

The central panel of this little triptych shows Mary with the child playing in the circle of virgin-martyrs. The left-hand wing shows St. Elizabeth with a beggar,

Master of the Deichsler Altar
(1st third of the 15th century)

8   Outer Sides of the Wings of the Deichsler Altar, c. 1415/20
Canvas on coniferous wood,
each wing 159.5 x 39.5 cm
Acquired 1844

and on the right is St. Agnes with the lamb. The virgins are identified by their names in the golden haloes and the attributes that they are given. St. Catherine of Alexandria, who was martyred under the emperor Maxentius, sits front left with a sword and wheel. Next to her is St. Dorothy, who wears roses in her hair and offers the Christ-child a basket of roses, which are symbolic of a miracle that occurred during her martyrdom. On the right is St. Margaret, identified by the cross with which she banished the Devil. Front right is St. Barbara with her tower on her knee; the tower reminds us that her father kept her prisoner in a tower before beheading her himself.

The four virgin-martyrs are members of the "virgines capitales", who were especially venerated by the faithful. They are sitting with Mary in a blossoming garden surrounded by a fence. Thus the location is identified as a "hortus con-clusus", where Mary and the Virgins enjoy the peace of the paradise garden, which is also promised to the faithful. Representations of the Mother of God in the garden of paradise were frequently produced around 1400.

This little altar was once intended for private worship and bears all the hallmarks of the master's style: bright, glowing colours, delicate doll-like heads and the gently flowing drapery that is characteristic of the "Soft Style" of "International Gothic". *RG*

Thuringian, c. 1430

10 Arnstadt Resurrection Altar
Fir wood with frame, central panel
142.7 x 147 cm,
left-hand wing 143 x 90.5 cm,
right-hand wing 143 x 55.7 cm
Acquired before 1922. Property of the
Kaiser Friedrich-Museums-Verein

The central panel shows Christ after he has risen from the open sarcophagus. He is wearing a crown, holding the flag of victory and raising his right hand. Two angels on the edge of the sarcophagus are proclaiming the resurrection of the Lord. The sleeping guardians of the tomb are resting in the foreground. On the left is Peter with the key and on the right Paul with the open book in his hand. God the Father, accompanied by three angels, has appeared in a garland of clouds before a starry sky. Mary is leading the three Marys to the tomb on the right-hand wing. The holy women are carrying boxes of ointment with which to anoint the Lord, and three angels are hovering above the holy women. On the left-hand wing ten apostles are kneeling to adore the risen Christ. Above them the Holy Spirit is descending from Heaven in the form of a dove. This pictorial presentation clearly deviates from the iconography of the resurrection. Sequential events are linked and fused into a single event. The inscriptions comment on the events, a device probably appropriated from medieval Easter plays. *RG*

Hans Multscher
(c. 1400 – before 1467)

11 The Wings of the Wurzach Altar
1437
Canvas on fir wood, each panel
150 x 140 cm
Acquired as a gift from Sir Julius Wernher,
London, 1900

These two altar-wings are among the most important works of German painting in the first half of the 15th century. In the 18th century they were in the collection of the Count of Waldburg-Zeil in Schloss Wurzach, hence the name *Wurzach Altar*.

The outer and inner sides of the wings, which were separated at an earlier period, show scenes from Christ's Passion and the Life of Mary arranged in two rows. The scenes of Christ's Passion were originally on the outside of the wings and could be seen for most of the year when the retable was closed.

There was probably a carved crucifix above them. The sequence of the Passion opens with *Christ on the Mount of Olives*. The disciples are huddled on the left, asleep, leaving Christ alone on watch. In the background the crowd of pursuers led by Judas is approaching. The subsequent scene, *Christ before Pilate*, is dominated by the rampant crowd, with Christ being pushed towards Pilate, who is seen washing his hands to signify that he is innocent of the death of the Lord. Next is *Christ Bearing the Cross* in which Christ strides forward, bent under the burden of the cross. He is followed by Simon of Cyrene, who was forced to help him. Mary, John and the women stand by helplessly, reviled and scorned by onlookers and soldiers. Children throwing stones accompany Christ on the way to the place of execution. The sequence concludes with the tranquil scene of the *Resurrection*. Christ ascends from the sealed sarcophagus, which is set in a rocky cave. He has raised his right

hand in blessing, and bears the banner of the cross in his left hand as a sign of victory. The sleeping watchmen are on the ground around the tomb.

The scenes from Mary's life, the inner sides of the wings, once flanked a shrine with large wood-carvings, which undoubtedly represented the Madonna surrounded by saints. They begin with the *Birth of Christ*. Mary and Joseph are kneeling beneath the roof of the stable, devoutly observing and worshipping the child. Outside in the field, the angel is proclaiming the Lord's birth to the shepherds. Men and women, whose faces express joy curiosity and amazement are crowded behind the wooden fence on the left. Next is the *Adoration of the Kings*. The Magi present the newborn king with gold, frankincense and myrrh in costly vessels. The age and appearance of the kings shows that in them all ages and all regions of the earth that were known at the time are bowing before Christ.

The Pentecostal Feast shows Mary in the centre of a circle with the twelve Apostles in a chapel-like room. Above them hovers the dove as a symbol of the Holy Spirit, which is being poured out over the faithful. Its rays form small tongues of fire above the heads of the solemn group. The *Death of Mary* is the concluding panel in this sequence. Mary's dead body lies on the bed around which the Apostles have gathered. Among them is Christ, who has taken Mary's soul to himself.

On the lower border of the Death of Mary is a line of lettering that looks as if it has been incised. It names Hans Multscher as the master responsible for the work and 1437 as the date of completion. Multscher, who worked in Ulm and was one of the leading artists of his day, is always described in sources as a sculptor. The question of whether he executed only the sculptures, now lost, or also the altar painting is therefore disputed.   *RG*

Konrad Witz (c. 1400 – before 1446)

12 The Queen of Sheba Before
Solomon, c. 1435/37
Oak, 84.5 x 79 cm
Acquired 1913

The Queen of Sheba's encounter with
King Solomon, which is recorded in the
Book of Kings, is one of eight scenes
depicted in the so-called Heilsspiegel
Altar, whose central section has not
survived. The work was presumably
intended for the church of St. Leonhard
in Basel. The inner sides of the wings
show scenes that were dealt with in
the "speculum humanae salvationis" or
Heilsspiegel (Mirror of Salvation), a devotional book of 14th-century Dominican mysticism. In this book, historical
and Old Testament events are related
typologically to God's working out of
salvation in history. This is based on
the idea that Christ's incarnation and
redemption of mankind was part of the
divine plan from the beginning. For
this reason events that occurred in the
distant past were always interpreted
as prefigurations of future events. The
Queen of Sheba's visit to Solomon,
whom she presented with gold and
spices, was seen in the Middle Ages as
the prefiguring of the Adoration of the
Kings, who also came from the East to
worship the Christ-child. For this
reason Christ was also seen as the new
Solomon. *RG*

Konrad Witz or his circle

13 Christ on the Cross, c. 1440/50
Wood, transferred to canvas, 34 x 26 cm
Acquired 1908

At first sight this small painting seems to
be a normal depiction of the Crucifixion, though one that has been transferred
to a wonderfully conceived north Alpine
landscape. However, the position of the
donor is surprising. He kneels in prayer
directly in front of Christ, while the biblical figures, Mary with two female saints
and St. John, are strangely placed behind
the cross. The solution is to be found by
looking at the cross itself, which with
its profiled base should obviously not be
regarded as the historic instrument of
the Passion on Golgotha but as a carved
wayside cross of the type that existed in
their thousands in central Europe. Accordingly the painting should be read
as showing the donor, who has fallen to
his knees in front of a roadside cross in
the evening on his way to the town that
is visible in the background. The reward
for the profundity of his meditation is
that Christ himself appears in place of
the carved crucifix, and the mourners
with him. We are seeing, as it were, the
personal vision of the donor, as he expe-
riences it in his home surroundings, by
a lake among the Swiss mountains. This
donor is a layman whose entirely red

clothing may be a reference to a particular office that he held—he is, however, not a cardinal, as is often assumed. The painter has superbly captured the evening mood on the lake and reproduced the atmosphere of haze in the distance and the passing clouds. The artist was either Konrad Witz himself, which would make this little panel his sole surviving small-format work, or an unknown painter from the immediate circle of the famous master from Basel. *SK*

Master of the Darmstadt Passion
(active c. 1450–1470)

14 Outer Sides of the Wings of a Crucifixion Altar, c. 1460
Coniferous wood, each panel 207 x 109 cm
Acquired with the Solly Collection, 1821

The four large panel pictures in the Berlin Gemäldegalerie were once the front and back parts to two altar wings. These were part of a monumental re-table, in the centre of which a populous

Calvary was to be seen. The outer sides of the wings show the Mother of God enthroned with the child and a clerical donor on the left, and the Holy Trinity on the right. God the Father is seated on the throne with his son's body on his lap. The depiction of the "Man of Sorrows" shows that the grace of God is revealed to man through the sacrifice of Christ.

The Master of the Darmstadt Passion was an extremely able artist who knew how to interweave light and colour and to use light to intensify the gentlest nuances of colour. Despite the enhanced realism of detail brought about by the luminous painting of the figures in his pictures, they still seem introverted and remarkably removed from reality. The fact that despite this restraint they are full of life and inner movement accounts for the particular charm of the great altar wings. They are an impressive document of the master's distinctive position as perhaps one of the greatest colourists of his age. *RG*

Salzburg School, c. 1480

15 The Trinity as the Throne of Mercy
Wood, 81 x 110 cm
Acquired 1937

God the Father is enthroned on clouds,
holding his Son, who has been taken
down from the cross, in his arms. Christ's
body bears the wounds of the Crucifixion, as witness of the Son of God's
sacrifice to redeem mankind. Six angels
hover around the group. Three of them
are presenting the tools of suffering or
"arma Christi". The double nature of
Christ, who is both God and man, is
shown by the fact that he is floating in
Heaven, but has his feet firmly on the
ground.

Mary and John are kneeling on the
ground. They have seized Christ's outspread arms so that they can kiss the
gaping wounds on his hands in quiet
mourning and profound worship. Mary
and John appear as mediators and inter-
cessors to be the Son of God's grace for
mankind. *RG*

Master of the Life of Mary
(active c. 1460/90)

16 Mary with the Child, c. 1470
Oak, with original frame, 57.5 x 50.5 cm
Acquired 1906. Property of the
Kaiser Friedrich-Museums-Verein

The Master of the Life of Mary, with the
Master of the Lyversberg Passion, made a
considerable contribution to painting in

Cologne in the second half of the 15th century. Contact with Netherlandish art gave new impetus to the master-painters who followed Stefan Lochner (c. 1400–1451). A stay in the Netherlands can thus be assumed as probable.

The Master of the Life of Mary stands out from this generally uniform group of artists for the delicacy and elegance of his pictorial figures. Traces of hinges on the left-hand side of the frame of this picture suggest that the panel was originally the right-hand half of a diptych.   RG

Master of the Housebook
(worked late 15th and early 16th century)

17   The Washing of the Apostles' Feet; The Last Supper, c. 1475/80
Coniferous wood,
each panel 131 x 75.6 cm
Acquired 1930

This master from the Central Rhine area is named after the "Hausbuch" in the possession of the Princes of Waldburg in Schloss Wolfegg—a collection of superb drawings whose subtlest works have been attributed to the Master of the Housebook.

The Washing of the Feet and *The Last Supper* formed the outer parts of the wings of the so-called Speyer Altar, whose various sections are now in museums in Freiburg, Frankfurt and Berlin.

The actual Passion begins with the washing of the feet. The disciples have assembled in a wood-panelled room before the Feast of the Passover; Christ is kneeling on the floor. The act of washing their feet is a symbol of love and humility.

The second scene shows *The Last Supper*, celebrated by the Lord as a farewell to his disciples on the evening before his death on the cross. The sky is bathed in reddish-yellow twilight, with clouds glowing in the last rays of the setting sun, showing a precise observation of nature.   RG

Martin Schongauer (c. 1475)

18 The Birth of Christ, c. 1480
Oak, 37.5 x 28 cm
Acquired 1902. Property of the
Kaiser Friedrich-Museums-Verein

Schongauer influenced German and
Netherlandish art well into the 16th
century, which underlines his unusual
impact. His importance to Albrecht
Dürer can scarcely be overestimated.
Schongauer's copperplate engravings
could be found all over Europe and
enjoyed universal acclaim. Over a
hundred engravings have survived, but
only very few paintings. *The Birth of
Christ* is probably one of the most
finished examples.

Mary kneels under the roof of the
dilapidated stable to worship the child,
who is lying on the floor. Behind her is
Joseph with folded hands. An ox and ass
also look upon the child. Animals were
seen as fulfilling Old Testament prophe-
cies, as the first witnesses to the Christ-
mas events, before the shepherds and
the Three Kings. The shepherds, having
approached from the right, are waiting
outside the stable, reverently and silently
worshipping the divine child.   *RG*

Master LCz   (active c. 1480–1510)

19 Christ before Pilate, c. 1500
Pine, 77.5 x 60 cm
Acquired 1917

This panel was part of a retable whose
parts are now dispersed around various museums. In the 19th century they
were in the collection of Dr. Strache of
Dornbach, near Vienna. The artist owes
this provenance to the name frequently
used by earlier researchers: "Master of the
Strache Altar".

Later scholars noticed a link with
copperplate engravings of the period
from 1492 to 1497, signed "LCz". The
master, who can be placed in Bamberg,
can presumably be identified as the
painter Lorenz Katzheimer, whom records show to have been there in 1505.
It is to be assumed that he trained in
Nuremberg. He is considered to be one
of the most striking Franconian painters
before Albrecht Dürer.

The other parts of the altar contain the following scenes: *Scourging*
(Paris, Louvre), *Crowning with Thorns*
(Nuremberg, Germanisches Nationalmuseum) and *Crucifixion of Christ*
(private collection). *Christ Praying on the
Mount of Olives* (Darmstadt, Hessisches
Landesmuseum) formed the central
panel of the retable.   *RG*

Master of the Aachen Altar
(active late 15th and early 16th century)

20 The Adoration of the Kings
c. 1510
Oak, 81 x 135 cm
Acquired 1917. Property of the
Kaiser Friedrich Museums Verein

Mary is seated at the centre of the picture in front of a rich brocade baldacchino supported by angels. The Three Kings
and their retinue approach on either side
to worship the child and to present him
with their gifts. Joseph, together with
the ox and ass, can be distinguished next
to the manger in the background of the
ruined stable. In the extreme foreground,
on a smaller scale, are male and female
donors with their coats of arms. The
painter, who came from the studio of the
Master of the Heilige Sippe, is an important exponent of early 16th-century
Cologne painting.   *RG*

Bernhard Strigel (c. 1460–1528)

21 Christ Taking Leave of his Mother,
c. 1520
Fir wood, 86.5 x 71.5 cm
Acquired 1850

Christ is embracing his mother outside
the Bethany town gate. She is bent over
in sorrow by the pain of leave-taking,
and clings to her son to prevent him
from going away. Mary's three companions are standing on the right by the gate.
Peter and two other apostles are waiting
for Christ under trees on the left. This
panel and the portrayal of the *Disrobing
of Christ*, also in the Gemäldegalerie,
were part of an extensive retable with
several sets of wings, said to come from
the church of St. Nicholas in Isny in
Allgäu. Strigel was court painter to
Emperor Maximilian I, and one of the
most notable late Gothic painters in
Swabia.   *RG*

Albrecht Dürer   (1471–1528)

22   The Madonna with the Siskin
1506
Poplar, 91 x 76 cm
Acquired 1893

Albrecht Dürer painted this picture for an unknown patron during his second visit to Venice in 1506. Mary is sitting with the child in front of a red curtain and behind her is a broad landscape filled with trees, ruins and distant hills. The naked child is playing with a siskin that has alighted on his arm. The bird symbolises the predestined Passion. The child holds a small sucker filled with sugar in his right band. Two cherubs are hovering over Mary and crowning her with a wreath of roses. The red and white flowers symbolise the pains and joys of the Mother of God. Her right hand is resting on an upright book; it is the Old Testament, whose prophesies have been fulfilled. On the right in the foreground are a youthful angel and the boy John. John is offering a bunch of lilies of the valley to the Mother of God as a symbol of her purity and virginity.

On the low table in the foreground is a piece of paper with Dürer's signature in Latin: "Albertus durer germanus faciebat post virginis partum 1506 AD". Dürer, in direct contact with the masters of the Italian Renaissance, is proudly asserting his German origins.   RG

Albrecht Dürer   (1471–1528)

23   Hieronymus Holzschuher, 1526
Lime, with original frame, 51 x 37 cm
Acquired 1884

This portrait was in Nuremberg until the late 19th century and owned by one of the subject's descendants. It is one of the most important portraits from Dürer's late period, dating from 1526. Holzschuher (1468–1529) was 57 years old at the time. He was a member of one of the most notable Nuremberg patrician families, which controlled the city. He was elected junior mayor in 1500 and senior mayor in 1509, joining the city's High Council as "Septemvir" in 1514. Dürer was a close friend of Holzschuher and brought presents back for him from his visit to Holland in 1521. The portrait is limited to the shoulders with their heavy fur collar and the impressive head, with the subject looking at the viewer. He is scrutinising the observer critically but with restrained sympathy.

The window frames of the room in which Dürer painted his friend's portrait are reflected in his eyes. The picture is still in the original frame, which has a sliding lid.   *RG*

status of the girl as an unmarried virgin. As there is no specific reference to the identity of the girl portrayed, the question has been raised of whether this may be not a portrayal of an actual person but an imagined head, a study of a type. However, both the expression and the features of this rather broad face seem rather to suggest that it is a portrait of a real young woman.   *SK*

Albrecht Dürer   (1471–1528)

24   Portrait of a Young Woman with a Red Beret, 1507
Vellum on wood, 30.4 x 20 cm
Acquired 1899. Property of the
Kaiser Friedrich-Museums-Verein

The portrait, which was probably painted immediately after Dürer's return from Venice in 1507, depicts a young woman dressed in the German manner. The beret worn with a slight tilt gives her a cheeky expression. The limitation of the colours of clothing to strawberry red and an intense green, which form a effective contrast to the tones of the skin and hair, lend this picture a particular charm. The jewellery on the beret, consisting of a ruby and pearl, signify wealth and a high social rank; the uncovered hair shows the

Hans Suess von Kulmbach
(c. 1480–1522)

25 The Adoration of the Kings, 1511
Lime, 153 x 110 cm
Acquired 1876

This busy composition was the central
panel of an altar that was presumably
intended for the monastery church of
na Skalce in Cracow, where parts of the
wings are still kept.

    Kulmbach trained in Dürer's studio.
He and Baldung were Dürer's most
important pupils. He lived and worked
as an independent master in Nuremberg
from 1511, when *The Adoration of the
Kings* was also painted. Mary is sitting
among the ruins of an ancient palace
with the child on her knee. The Three
Kings are approaching her with a colourful retinue. Above them is the star that
the kings followed to Bethlehem.
On the right is a view through an
archway into a broad landscape bathed
in sunshine, from which riders are
approaching on horses and camels. Some
of them are in Polish national dress, with
characteristically laced coats and high
caps trimmed with fur. *RG*

Hans Baldung, called Grien
(1484/85–1545)

26 Ludwig Graf of Löwenstein 1513
Lime, 48 x 34 cm
Acquired 1918. Property of the
Kaiser Friedrich-Museums-Verein

This portrait shows the subject's head,
shoulders and left arm. He is wearing a
red biretta and a black greatcoat decorated with strips of gold brocade. He is
holding on to the fur of his collar with
his left hand, a gesture expressing his
decisive qualities. The striking features
are evidence of energy and awareness
of his own power. The subject was born
on 29 September, 1463, as the illegiti-
mate son of Elector Friedrich I of the
Palatinate and Clara Tott, the daughter
of a bourgeois family in Augsburg. His
cousin, Philip the Magnanimous, transferred the county of Löwenstein in the
Neckar area over to him in 1488, along
with other estates. Emperor Maximilian I
made him Count of Löwenstein in 1494.
He later became an Imperial War Coun-
cillor and undertook numerous diplomatic missions. He died, having probably
been murdered, on 28 March, 1524. This
portrait was painted during Baldung's
visit to the Neckar area. *RG*

Hans Baldung, called Grien
(1484/85–1545)

27   The Altar of the Three Kings
c. 1506/07
Lime, central panel 121 x 70 cm,
each wing 121 x 28 cm
Acquired 1872

From 1503 onwards, Baldung spent some
years in Albrecht Dürer's studio. Shortly
after this he received his first major commission. This was for two altars, probably
intended for the Liebfrauenkirche in
Halle on the Saale. These were *The Altar
of the Three Kings* and *The Sebastian Altar*
in Nuremberg, dated 1507 (Germanisches Nationalmuseum). They were
presumably commissioned by Ernst von
Wettin, Archbishop of Magdeburg and
Bishop of Halle, brother to the Saxon
Elector Friedrich the Wise.

   The Altar of the Three Kings is a tri-
partite folding altar with movable wings
that were separated later. The outer sides
show SS. Catherine and Agnes.

   The Adoration of the Kings is portrayed

in the central panel of the feast-day side.
The king standing in the centre and
staring insistently at the viewer presumably represents the donor. His portrait
is also to be found in *The Sebastian Altar*
in Nuremberg. Two knight-saints are
portrayed on the inner sides of the wings
alongside the central panel. On the left
is St. George with the dragon at his feet.
According to legend he killed the monster and thus freed a princess. The saint
was considered the patron of all knights
and warriors. Opposite him is St. Mau-
rice, who was the leader of the Theban
Legion and later a martyr. He was particularly venerated in Halle as patron of the
archbishopric. For this reason the fortress
built by Archbishop Ernst, the presumed
donor of the altar, is called the Moritz-
burg. The principal features of this work
are the glowing colours and a preference
for portraying costly fabrics and shining
armour.   RG

Hans Baldung, called Grien
(1484/85–1545)

28 The Lamentation of Christ
c. 1516
Lime, 141.3 x 96 cm
Acquired 1907

The body of Christ, covered with wounds, lies at the foot of the cross, close to the viewer. Behind him sits the sor-rowful Mother of God. John has moved the body into a half-sitting position and is supporting the head, which is leaning sideways. Mary Magdalene tenderly holds Christ's hand to her cheek. The group is completed by Joseph of Arimathaea, who is holding a vessel of ointment. The composition is alive with power-ful creative force. An impressive feature is Christ's athletic body, bearing all the marks of torture and death. This shows the influence of Matthias Grünewald, who had depicted the tormented saviour with ruthless realism a few years before, in the Isenheim altarpiece. *RG*

Hans Baldung, called Grien
(1484/85–1545)

29 Pyramus and Thisbe, c. 1530
Lime, 92.6 x 69.5 cm
Acquired 1920

The subject of the picture is the dramatic story of Pyramus and Thisbe, handed down by the Roman author Ovid in his *Metamorphoses*. It is about two children who were neighbours in Babylon and their unhappy love. They arranged to meet, against their parents' will, at a well outside the city. On the way there Thisbe encountered a lioness who had come to the well to quench its thirst after hunting. Thisbe ran away from the animal, losing her veil in the process. The lioness tore it to pieces, and stained it with the blood of its prey. When Pyramus reached the well he found the lioness's tracks and the bloody veil. Convinced that his beloved had been killed by the lioness, he killed himself with his own sword. Thisbe came back to the meeting-place and found her dying lover there. She realised how the tragedy had happened, and she too committed suicide. *RG*

of a double portrait. The image of the nobleman that formed the other half, now located in Nuremberg, depicts a man wearing a lawyer's gown from the University of Vienna. He was formerly identified as Stephan Reuss, the Rector of the University, but recent research has ruled this out. *RG*

Lucas Cranach the Elder
(1472–1553)

30 Portrait of a Scholar's Wife, 1503
Coniferous wood, 52.5 x 36.5 cm
Acquired 1923

A middle-aged woman is sitting with an open landscape behind her. She is wearing a dress that is lavishly decorated with gold brocade and a white bonnet. In the background are two trees, one with and one without leaves—symbolic of the woman's past and future. Cranach painted her in a realistic fashion, without hiding the first signs of ageing. This painting was originally one half

parrot for the Christ Child. Still more angels are singing or drawing water from the well that, according to legend, sprang up where the Holy Family rested. Joseph is standing by Mary, wearing a hat and with his staff in his hands. The large numbers of flowering plants give the resting-place the solitude of paradise. Many of the plants have a symbolic significance and relate to Mary and Christ.   *RG*

Lucas Cranach the Elder
(1472–1553)

32 Altarpiece with the Last Judgement, c. 1524
Lime, central panel 163 x 125 cm,
each wing 163 x 58 cm
Acquired from the Royal Palaces, 1829

Christ is enthroned as Judge of the World over a nocturnal landscape bright with the light of fires. The dead have risen at the trumpet's call on the Day of Judgement. Devils have taken over the world, in order to torture sinners and prepare unimaginable torments for them. The left-hand wing shows the world at the beginning of creation. The Creation of Eve, the Fall of Man and the Expulsion from Paradise are shown in a broad, sunny landscape. The altar is a copy of Hieronymus Bosch's triptych, now in Vienna.   *RG*

Lucas Cranach the Elder
(1472–1553)

31 Rest on the Flight to Egypt, 1504
Beechwood, 70.7 x 53 cm
Acquired 1902

The Holy Family, fleeing from Herod's men, has settled down on a grassy slope under an ancient grey fir tree. Mary is sitting on the verge and holding the child on her lap. He is playfully reaching for a strawberry plant that a small angel is offering him. Another angel has caught a

Venus, the goddess of beauty and love, turns her upper body slightly towards the viewer. She is adorned with costly chains and rings in gold and precious stones. Venus's son Cupid is standing beside her on a low plinth, with his bow and arrow in his hands. Cranach, who often turned to this subject, has added an earlier version of a Latin inscription in which the viewer is warned and enjoined to beware of the temptations of love, so that Venus cannot hold him in her power.   *RG*

Lucas Cranach the Elder
(1472–1553)

33 David and Bathsheba, 1526
Beechwood, 38.8 x 25.7 cm
Acquired 1890

According to the Second Book of Samuel, King David caught a glimpse of Bathsheba, the wife of his soldier Uria, one evening while she was bathing. The king fell in love and committed adultery with her. But he sent Uria to war, arranged for him to be killed in battle and married Bathsheba. In the Middle Ages the story of David and Bathsheba was seen as a warning of women's power over men. This small picture, which depicts the biblical story as a contemporary event, was probably painted as a collector's piece for a prince's chamber of art treasures.   *RG*

Lucas Cranach the Elder
(1472–1553)

34 Venus and Cupid, c. 1530
Fir wood, 167 x 62 cm
From the Royal Palaces, 1829

Lucas Cranach the Elder
(1472–1553)

35 The Fountain of Youth, 1546
Lime, 122.5 x 186.5 cm
Acquired from the Royal Palaces, 1829

Like a theatrical play, Cranach staged his painting on the theme of man's longing for immortality and eternal youth. Man dreams of being able to leave his spent mortal frame, emerging rejuvenated, fresh and ready for action. The idea of the purifying forces of the elements, fire and water, is as old as mankind itself.

The image is centred around the so-called "Fountain of Youth". It is set in a detailed landscape, far from human settlements. The course of events is read from left to right.

Old, frail women are brought along stony paths from the left, coming from a barren, rocky landscape. They come in carriages or carts, are carried, or make their own painful way, sustained by hope, to the pool. Others are being undressed and examined by the doctor. Some hesitate, or need to be persuaded. In the water itself they become visibly younger, and climb out on the right-hand side, fresh and youthful in form.

Here they are received by a cavalier and taken to a tent, where they are dressed again. After this they devote themselves to the joys of life, in new garments and festively adorned. All this cheerful activity, with eating, dancing, music and playful love takes place in a blossoming landscape. This is the home of eternal youth.

On the left-hand side one is reminded of old age and its complaints, symbolised by the barren rocky wilderness. Thus the elements of the landscape relate entirely to the events of the picture, and are subordinated to them.

The figures of Venus and Cupid can be seen on the fountain in the pool, indicating that this is a fountain of love: the miracle-working power of love is the actual source of eternal youth. But it appears that only women need to bathe in the pool: the men rejuvenate themselves through contact with the women.

Lucas Cranach reinterpreted the old theme of the fountain of youth entirely in the spirit of the courtly taste of his princely patrons, turning it into a fountain of love, or of Venus.   *RG*

Hans Burgkmair
(1473–1531)

36 The Birth of Christ, 1511
Lime, 45 x 33 cm
Acquired 1843

The Augsburg artist painted the Holy Family in a close-up composition, a depiction which due to the place shown and the auxiliary scene of the Annunciation to the Shepherds is extended to the theme of the Nativity. Mary seems to be sitting like a queen on a throne, with her little son in her lap. The child turns to her for assistance, while from the left his adoptive father Joseph comes with grapes. In a prefiguration of the Passion of Christ, the grapes have alarmed the child, who is still a baby but at the same time is divine too and already knows his fate on earth. The stable in the background, which also serves as an ennobling architectural backdrop for the Virgin, is represented as an antique ruin. In artistic terms Burgkmair's architecture is testimony to his study of the Italian Renaissance, which he was one of the first painters in Germany to undertake. The Alpine like landscape in turn is a reference to models from places to the north of Italy, possibly the early works of Albrecht Altdorfer.   *SK*

The star, surrounded by a brightly glowing aureole, remains above the stable in Bethlehem and illuminates the darkness of the night. Alongside it, three angels hover in the sky singing the "Gloria". Another has appeared in a cloud of light in the background on the left, in order to proclaim the joyful birth of Christ to a shepherd in the field. The little picture is filled with celestial light, reflected in the foliage on the tree, the dilapidated stable walls and even the grass on the ground. It is a dream-like, mysterious mood that shifts the events of the holy night away from reality.   *RG*

Albrecht Altdorfer
(c. 1480–1538)

37 The Birth of Christ, c. 1513
Lime, 36.6 x 26 cm
Acquired 1892

The Holy Family, almost hidden, has found makeshift shelter in the lower storey of the ruined stable. Mary and Joseph are worshipping the child, which is carried in a cloth by three angels. Joseph holds his hand around the candle-flame to prevent it from being blown out by the draught. In fact this is intended to indicate that the celestial light of the divine child completely outshines the glow of the earthly light.

Albrecht Altdorfer (c. 1480–1538)

38   Rest on the Flight to Egypt, 1510
Lime, 57 x 38 cm
Acquired 1876

The Holy Family is resting on its flight
from pursuers sent by Herod in front of
a fantastic mountain landscape on the
banks of a great expanse of water. Mary
is sitting on a throne next to a lavishly

decorated Renaissance fountain, supporting the boy Jesus with her arm. Joseph
is arriving from the right and presenting
Mary with cherries. The Latin inscription on the panel in front of the fountain
base states that Albrecht Altdorfer of Regensburg piously dedicated the picture to
the divine Mary for the salvation of his
soul.   *RG*

Albrecht Altdorfer (c. 1480–1538)

39 Christ on the Cross between the
Two Thieves, c. 1526
Lime, 28.7 x 20.8 cm
Acquired 1886

The crosses of Christ and the thieves
are at the top of a hill in an open landscape. Gloomy clouds have swept in and
obscured the sun. Christ has died. The
curious onlookers have departed and the
executioners and soldiers have dispersed.
In the foreground John and Joseph of
Arimathaea are helping the Mother of
God and one of the women away. Nico-
demus and a servant are leaning a ladder
against the cross so that they can take
down the body. Mary Magdalene
is sitting in the foreground. She holds
her head in her hand as she mourns.
The cosmic dimension of Christ's crucifixion is reflected in the dramatic light in
the sky. *RG*

Albrecht Altdorfer (c. 1480–1538)

40 Allegory. Begging Sits on Pride's
Train, 1531
Lime, 28.7 x 41 cm
Acquired 1876

A richly dressed nobleman and his wife
are walking up steps to the terrace of
a palace. There a cavalier is waiting for
them with a magnificent goblet from
which to toast their arrival. A family of
beggars has settled down on the end of
the long train, and the noble couple are
unwittingly pulling them along behind.
The title of the picture vividly captures
the core of the allegory, which could
also be slightly altered as "Pride Goeth
Before a Fall". *RG*

Wolf Huber   (1480/85–1553)

41   The Rest on the Flight to Egypt
c. 1525/30
Lime, 56.2 x 55.6 cm
Loan from the Kunstbibliothek, SMPK

Mary is riding on an ass and holding the
child in swaddling clothes solicitously in
her arms. Joseph is leading her mount
and striding securely ahead on the uncertain path. An ox on a rope is trotting
behind them with its eyes wide open.
The path leads the travellers through a
lonely mountain forest. A many-towered
city is spread out on the banks of a lake
deep in the valley. Icy mountain sum-
mits thrust upwards in the distance. The
terrain seems barren and uninviting.
Nevertheless the rays of the morning
sun, shining on the forest floor and on
the trees, convey an impression of profound peace. The break of the young day
awakens hope of a happy end to the
dangerous journey.   *RG*

Master LS   (active 1st half of the
16th century)

42   Portrait of a Herr Rehlinger, 1540
Lime, 46 x 48 cm
Acquired with the Solly Collection, 1821

This is a portrait of a young man in costly tournament armour. The coat of arms

on his finger ring identifies the subject as a member of the patrician Rehlinger family, whose seat was in Hainhofen near Augsburg. The lavish and highly typical ornamentation on the etched and fluted armour indicates work by the Augsburg etcher-painter Jörg Sorg the Elder, who is in the records as a master from 1517. At the throat the armour bears the date 1527, which can also be presumed to be the year when the painting was completed. On stylistic grounds a triptych of approximately the same date can be attributed to the painter of this portrait. This triptych, the so-called University Altar, also originated in Augsburg and is today in the Alte Pinakothek in Munich. RG

Christoph Amberger
(c. 1500–1561/62)

43 Sebastian Münster, c. 1552
Lime, 54 x 42 cm
Acquired 1819

A 16th-century inscription on the back of the panel provides information about the subject. It says: "Sebastian Münster Cosmographus. Painted at the age of 65, Ao. 1552". Sebastian Münster was born in 1488 in Ingelheim in Rhine-Hesse, entered the Franciscan Order as a young man and then studied in Heidelberg, Louvain and Tübingen. Later he dedicated himself to the Reformation. He was a teacher and professor, subsequently becoming Rector of the University of Basel, where he died in 1552. Münster's fame was based on the *Cosmographia Universalis*, a comprehensive description of the world in six volumes, which appeared in new editions well into the 17th century. RG

Hans Holbein the Younger
(1497–1543)

44 Duke Anton the Good of Lorraine, c. 1543
Oak, 51 x 37 cm
Acquired 1897

The subject is Duke Anton the Good of Lorraine (1489–1544), a faithful follower of the French king François I. He took part in the latter's Italian campaign in 1515, and was involved in the conquest of Milan. The portrait shows him at age 54, wearing a doublet with red sleeves, a black greatcoat and a biretta with gold laces. There is no status symbol revealing his rank. The fact that Holbein restricts himself to the essentials and the balanced colour tones indicate that this portrait dates from his late period. It may be one of the artist's last works. RG

Hans Holbein the Younger
(1497–1543)

45 The Merchant Georg Gisze, 1532
Oak, 96.3 x 85.7 cm
Acquired with the Solly Collection, 1821

The portrait shows the Hanseatic merchant from Gdansk, Georg Gisze (1497–1562), at age 34, sitting behind a writing table in a corner of his London office, surrounded by numerous objects that identify his rank. On the table in front of him are his writing implements and a gold time-piece, and also a glass vase with carnations, sprigs of rosemary, basil and wallflowers. The vase and flowers are symbolic of the subject's qualities: his unwavering love, faithfulness, purity and modesty. The clock is a reminder of the passage of time and the fading flowers indicate the brevity of life, while the fragility of the glass indicates that even the most beautiful things in life do not last for ever. In 1532, the year the portrait was painted, Georg Gisze was one of the leading men in the London Stalhof, one of the Hanseatic League's most powerful trade bases.   *RG*

French, c. 1400

46 The Coronation of Our Lady
Oak, circular, diameter 20.5 cm
Acquired 1906. Property of the
Kaiser Friedrich-Museums-Verein

Christ is sitting on a stone throne with the globe in his hand and crowning Mary, who kneels before him accompanied by two angels. The arrangement of the figures and the faces of Mary and the angels are reminiscent of miniatures in

case, this might have been the Duke of Burgundy, John the Fearless († 1419), as the canvas painting has a close stylistic connection to the work of Jean Malouel, Duke John's court painter.   *RG*

Jan van Eyck (c. 1390–1441)

48 The Crucifixion of Christ,
c. 1430/35
Wood, transferred to canvas, 43 x 26 cm
Acquired 1897

the prayer books made for the Duc de Berry (d. 1416). Thus this small circular picture is attributed to an artist who was a successor to André Beauneveu (d. 1401/02), who worked for the duke in Bourges.   *RG*

French, c. 1410

47 Madonna with Angels
Canvas, 107 x 81 cm
Acquired 1987

This painting is one of the earliest surviving paintings on canvas. The conspicuous gesture of the infant Christ, who looks to the left, could be a reference to the existence of a second painting with a praying donor on that side. If that is the

Christ is hanging heavily, an enormous figure between his mother Mary and his favourite disciple John. Their gestures and expressions reveal intense sorrow; their eyes are red from weeping. Beyond the stony place of crucifixion rises many-towered Jerusalem with the massive temple, on the left next to Christ. The freshly observed landscape with a detailed view of the city, distant mountain ranges partly covered in snow, and countless details in the middle ground—including crossing paths, bare trees and a windmill—testify to the outstanding quality of the painting, which however suffered a great deal when it was transferred to canvas in the 19th century. Because of its stylistic closeness to the Ghent Altarpiece of 1432, this panel is likely to be an early work by Jan van Eyck.   *SK*

The light, penetrating the church from the north, also refers to the supernatural significance of all things. The ambiguity of the picture is appropriate to Christian thinking in the late Middle Ages. Thus architecture, light and the altar indicate Mary's priestly role and her quality as the house of God and temple of Christ. *RG*

Jan van Eyck (c. 1390–1441)

50 Baudouin de Lannoy, c. 1435/40
Oak, 26 x 19.5 cm
Acquired 1902

Baudouin de Lannoy (1388–1474) was a high-ranking aristocrat in the Burgundian Netherlands. He was admitted to the Order of the Golden Fleece, the most exclusive chivalric order in Europe, as early as 1430, in the year the order was founded. In this portrait he has laid the chain of the order over his expensive coat of gold brocade. The facial expression of this approximately fifty-year-old man was clearly intended to express the firmness of purpose and decisiveness of a strict aristocrat. The painter has rendered the features of the subject, which are characteristic though far from the ideal of beauty, with great precision, and recorded the differing colorations and variations of the skin and the character of the materials. *SK*

Jan van Eyck (c. 1390–1441)

49 The Madonna in the Church
c. 1440
Oak, 31 x 14 cm
Acquired with the Suermondt Collection, 1874

Mary is standing in the nave of a Gothic cathedral, larger than life, and with the child. The detailed depiction of the architecture and the subtle grading of the light give the church interior a spatial aura that is all its own. The bright daylight coming in through the lead-framed clerestory windows and the side portal is a reminder of the passage of time.

The recorded inscription on the frame, which has not survived, praised the miracle of Christ's birth and Mary's virginity. The sunlight, which penetrates the windows without destroying them, also relates allegorically to Mary, who was a mother and yet remained a virgin.

Master of Flémalle

51 Portrait of a Fat Man, c. 1435/40
Oak, 28.5 x 17.7 cm
Acquired 1901. Property of the
Kaiser Friedrich-Museums-Verein

Filling the frame, the head of this unknown man has astonishing presence.
The bulk of the fleshy cheeks has great
immediacy, but the alert look in the eyes
with their stylised rendering lends the
portrait a quality that goes beyond cor-
pulence. The person portrayed and his
painter, who was probably from the
circle of Rogier van der Weyden, aim to
create a dignified portrait: the heaviness
of the features makes the man recognisable as an individual, but his look is
intended to express qualities of mind
which could possibly be described as
good judgement and reason, and certainly as piety too. *SK*

Petrus Christus (c. 1410–1472/73)

52 Mary with the Child,
St. Barbara and a Carthusian Monk
(Exeter Madonna), c. 1450
Oak, 19.5 x 14 cm
Acquired 1888

This small panel shows the donor in the
white vestments of the Carthusian Order, with the habit belted at the hip and
cloak-like scapular. He is presumably Jan
Vos, who was prior of the Carthusian
monastery of Genadedal near Bruges
from 1441 to 1450, and after that was
appointed prior of the monastery of
Nieuwlicht near Utrecht. He is kneeling
to worship the Madonna, who has the
child in her arms. The child has raised
his right hand in blessing, and is holding
a crystal globe in his left hand as a sign
of his rule over the whole world. Behind
the donor is St. Barbara, identified by
her attribute of a tower. She holds the
martyr's palm in her right hand, and is
touching the donor's shoulder with the
same hand. The scene is set in a hall with
lead-glazed windows, and open arches
look out as if from a vantage-point over
a vast open landscape with hills, woods,
meadows and a town by the river. *RG*

Petrus Christus
(c. 1410–1472/73)

53 Two Wings of a Triptych, 1452
Oak, each panel 134 x 56 cm
Acquired 1850

These altar wings date from 1452 and carry the signature "petrus xpi", made up of Latin and Greek letters. The artist became a citizen of Bruges on 6 July, 1444, and was repeatedly mentioned in documents between 1454 and 1472. Petrus Christus, who built on the achievements of Jan van Eyck, Robert Campin and Rogier van der Weyden, achieved his distinct position in Netherlandish painting because of his new combination of the figure and space. These two altar wings were part of a retable whose central section presumably showed a scene from Christ's Passion. The left-hand wing is divided into two parts. The upper half shows the Annunciation to Mary. Under this the Birth of Christ is to be seen, and Mary and Joseph are worshipping the child. Salome is kneeling in the foreground on the right; she doubted the virgin birth and was converted by a miracle. The composition shows clear analogies with Robert Campin's *Birth of Christ* in Dijon. The right-hand wing shows the Last Judgement, in which Christ is enthroned above the rainbow as judge of the world. On earth, the Archangel Michael is fighting against death and the Devil. This is an imaginative copy of a work on the same theme attributed to Jan van Eyck in the Metropolitan Museum of Art in New York. *RG*

Petrus Christus
(c. 1410–1472/73)

54 Portrait of a Young Woman
c. 1470
Oak, 29 x 22.5 cm
Acquired with the Solly Collection, 1821

Petrus Christus's portraits are the first
in Netherlandish painting to show the
subject in concrete spatial surroundings,
which adds a great deal to the immediacy of their appearance. Neither Rogier
van der Weyden nor Jan van Eyck took
the opportunity of presenting the subject
in appropriate surroundings.   RG

Rogier van der Weyden
(1399/1400–1464)

55 The Altar of Our Lady, before 1445
Oak, each panel 71 x 43 cm
Acquired 1850

The painted architecture is reminiscent
of the portals of Gothic cathedrals. It
defines the pictorial space as a place for
sacred events. Painted reliefs, with scenes
from the lives of Christ and Mary in the
hollow moulding of the portals, place
the events portrayed beneath them in
the chronology of the history of salvation. Events from the Old Testament on
the column capitals help to interpret
the principal scenes. The left-hand panel
shows Mary worshipping the child, who
is lying in her lap. She is sitting humbly
on the floor. Joseph is at her side, leaning on his staff, his head bent slightly
forward in sleep. The central panel shows
the Lamentation of Christ. Mary is holding the body of Christ in both arms,
and Joseph of Arimathaea and John are
standing beside her. The empty cross
rises behind them. The right-hand panel
shows the risen Christ appearing to his
mother, to comfort her and to tell her
about his bodily resurrection. These three
events bear witness to Mary's role in the
work of redemption. Angels with crowns
and banderoles praising the virtues of the
Mother of God hover at the apex of the
portals.   RG

Rogier van der Weyden
(1399/1400–1464)

56 The Middelburg Altar, c. 1445–50
Oak, central panel 91 x 89 cm,
each wing 91 x 40 cm
Acquired 1834

The central panel shows the birth of
Christ with the donor worshipping the
child, who is lying on the floor of the
stable, with a bright light around him.
The Romanesque architectural forms of
the building make it clear that the appearance of Christ brought a new era.
Joseph is protecting the candle-flame to
show that all earthly light is outshone
by the divine child. On the right-hand
panel the Three Magi are kneeling before the divine child. The left-hand panel
shows Emperor Augustus, the ruler of
the Western world, accompanied by a
prophetess, kneeling to the vision of the
Madonna. The triptych thus encompasses
the whole world in that the rulers of the
East and the West submit to the infant
Christ, the King of Kings.   *RG*

Rogier van der Weyden
(1399/1400–1464)

57 Portrait of a Woman with a
Winged Bonnet, c. 1440/1445
Oak, 47 x 32 cm
Acquired 1908

This may be the earliest surviving portrait by Rogier van der Weyden, and

is probably also his liveliest, due to the
woman's open look, directed straight at
the viewer, and the intelligent, almost
challenging expression in her face. Her
hands and the details of her clothing
have been painted with intense precision.
These details, and equally the composition, reveal the inspiration of Jan van
Eyck, which was very marked in the art
of Rogier in the period around 1440.
The identity of the young woman is
unknown. Her bonnet shows her to be
a married woman; the superior but not
luxurious clothing indicates a woman
from the middle class, who may have
lived in Brussels.   *SK*

Rogier van der Weyden
(1399/1400–1464)

58 The Altar of St. John, c. 1455
Oak, each panel 77 x 48 cm
Acquired 1850

The Altar of St. John, in its basic disposi-
tion, is linked with the *Miraflores Altar*.
The presentation starts on the left-hand
panel with the birth and naming of St.
John. The centre of the retable is taken
up by the Baptism of Christ, as the most
important event in terms of God's plan
of salvation. The third panel shows the
beheading of St. John. Statues of the
twelve Apostles are seen in the niches of
the painted frames. In the archivolts are
scenes from the lives of Christ and St.
John, which further link the main scenes
with the history of salvation.   RG

Jacques Daret   (c. 1400/03–1466)

59   The Visitation of Mary;
The Adoration of the Kings, 1434/35
Oak, each panel 57 x 52 cm
Acquired with the Solly Collection, 1821

Daret was trained in Tournai by Robert
Campin and later worked for the abbey of St. Vaast in Arras. Daret's few surviving works include four paintings which
formed the outer sides of the wings of an
altar that he painted in 1434/35 for the
Arras monastery church. The altar was
commissioned by Jean du Clercq, who
was abbot of the monastery from 1428
to 1462. Aside from *The Visitation of Mary*
and *The Adoration of the Kings*, the other
surviving works are *The Birth of Christ*
(Thyssen-Bornemisza Museum, Madrid)
and *The Presentation in the Temple* (Musée
du Petit Palais, Paris).   RG

Simon Marmion   (c. 1435–489)

60   The Wings of the Saint-Omer
Retable: Scenes from the Life of
St. Bertin, c. 1459
Oak, each panel 56 x 147 cm
Acquired 1905

Simon Marmion is one of the outstanding French masters in the second half of
the 15th century. This retable with wings
by Marmion used to be in the Benedictine abbey of St. Bertin in Saint-Omer.
The altar was consecrated in 1459, and
was commissioned by Bishop Guillaume
Fillastre (d. 1473), abbot of St. Bertin
and advisor to Duke Philip the Good of
Burgundy.

The central part of the shrine was
destroyed in the late 18th century. The
battlement-like tops of the wings were
separated in the 19th century and are
now in London (National Gallery). The
wing's inner panels show the donor in
bishop's vestments and nine scenes from
the life of St. Bertin (d. 698), including

the birth of the saint, his clothing cer-
emony at the monastery of Luxeuil and
his reception by St. Omer, followed by
the foundation and building of the new
monastery.

The right-hand wing starts with the
wine miracle legend; an empty barrel had
filled up with wine of its own accord.
As a result of this a knight who had
fallen of his horse was healed, and subsequently entered the monastery. Later four
Breton nobleman were also taken into
the order. The cycle of pictures ends with
the saint's temptation and death.

The brilliant colours and wealth of
detail demonstrate Marmion's considerable skill as a miniaturist. His handling
of light, which is accentuated in the
architecture and gives the rooms their
distinct atmosphere, is particularly
remarkable.   *RG*

Jean Fouquet   (c. 1420 – c. 1480)

61   Étienne Chevalier with
St. Stephen, c. 1454/56
Oak, 93 x 85 cm
Acquired 1896

This panel was originally the left-hand
half of a diptych in the cathedral of
Notre Dame de Melun, placed over
the tomb of the founder's wife. The
corresponding right-hand wing with
a depiction of the Madonna is now in
Antwerp. The founder, Étienne Chevalier
(d. 1474), is kneeling in the foreground,
accompanied by his patron saint, St.
Stephen. The sharp-edged stone on the
book in his hand refers to the stoning by
which the martyr met his death. Étienne

Chevalier was ambassador and chancellor under Charles VII and Louis XI of France and was entrusted with numerous diplomatic missions. In 1463, he was sent to Lille to redeem the cities on the Somme from fiefdom to Burgundy.   *RG*

Dieric Bouts   (1410/20–1475)

62   Christ at the House of Simon the Pharisee, c. 1460
Oak, 40.5 x 61 cm
Acquired 1904

The fascination exercised by Dieric Bout's work is based on his considerable ability to convey a sense of space, acquired from his training in the northern Netherlands and close acquaintance with the work of Petrus Christus and Rogier van der Weyden. Space plays a dominant role, stationing the figures in the pictures precisely and allowing no changes as a static element; thus time is eliminated as well. The event portrayed is based on St. Luke's Gospel (7, 36-50), according to which Christ was a guest in the house of Simon the Pharisee. Mary Magdalene, a reputed sinner, appeared during the meal and knelt before Christ, bathed his feet in tears, anointed them with oil, and then dried them with her hair, gaining forgiveness for all her sins from this show of repentance.   *RG*

Aelbert van Ouwater
(c. 1415– c. 1475)

63   The Raising of Lazarus
c.1450/60
Oak, 122 x 92 cm
Acquired 1889

Little is known about the life of this
master. From a stylistic point of view, he
is closely related to Jan van Eyck, Petrus
Christus and Dieric Bouts. Ouwater
is considered to be one of the leading
painters of his time in the northern
Netherlands.

According to the Gospel of St. John
(11,1–45), Christ brought Lazarus back
to life after he had been buried in a
sealed tomb for four days. Placing the
event in the choir of a Romanesque
church is intended to show that the Old
Testament period is ended by the age
of the Messiah. Thus Christ's words are
central to the work's statement: "I am
the resurrection and the life. He who
believes in me, though he die, yet shall
he live" (John 11, 25). This is the only
surviving work by the artist, and it was in
the church of St. Bavo in Haarlem until
1573.   RG

Hugo van der Goes
(c. 1440–1482)

64   The Adoration of the Kings
(Monforte Altar), c. 1470
Oak, 147 x 242 cm
Acquired 1914

Hugo van der Goes is assumed to have
been born in Ghent. In 1467 he was
accepted by the city's painters' guild as
a free master and, by 1473, he was dean
of the guild. At the height of his fame,
in 1477, he retreated to the monastery
of Roodendaele near Brussels. Despite
the severe mental illness that clouded
his later years he continued to work as
a painter.

Van der Goes's artistic achievement
is all the more remarkable because his
entire output is concentrated within a
period of only fifteen years. He produced works of art that are among the
most remarkable achievements of late
15th-century Netherlandish art in their
expressive and monumental qualities.

The Adoration of the Kings was the central panel to a large triptych. Old copies
show that the wings depicted the birth
and circumcision of Christ. The work's
altered state can be seen from the loss of
the wings, and the fact that the central
panel has been cut down: it used to have
a raised rectangular section in the centre.

The altar's appellation derives from
its stay in the monastery of Monforte de
Lemos in northern Spain, where it was
presumably taken in the 16th century.
The patron and the altar's original purpose are unknown.

The Adoration of the Kings is one of
Hugo van der Goes's earliest large works.
Mary is sitting in front of a palace-like
building with the child on her lap. Joseph
is kneeling beside her, greeting the kings
from the East. These representatives of
the three realms of the world have gathered reverently with their gifts to pay
tribute to the new ruler of the world.

The figures in the picture are true
to life to an extent that goes far beyond
anything achieved in Netherlandish art
until that time. The theme of the Adoration has seldom been so movingly recre-
ated. The rendering of the costly fabrics
and objects, the richness of the colours
and the immediacy of the event give this
part of the mystery of salvation a closeness to the present that its contemporary
viewers must have perceived as a sign
of the living significance of the events
portrayed.   *RG*

Hugo van der Goes
(c. 1440–1482)

65 The Adoration of the Shepherds
c. 1480
Oak, 97 x 245 cm
Acquired 1903

This painting dates from the artist's
last creative period. *The Adoration of the
Shepherds* has been identified on various
occasions as a predella, i.e. the lower
part of an altarpiece, but this is unlikely
for various reasons. Mary and Joseph are
kneeling on either side of the manger,
surrounded by the angels who are
worshipping the child with them. The
shepherds to whom God's angel has
proclaimed the birth of Christ come
hurrying in from the left, curious and
full of joy. When confronted with this
miracle taking place before their eyes
they kneel down or stop in a running
pose with their mouths wide open. The
picture is framed on the right and left
by two large half-length figures who are
drawing a curtain aside. These are Old
Testament prophets, who had foretold
Christ's birth. They underline the profound significance of the event, as they
had proclaimed that God would be made
man. The sheaf of corn by the manger
is vividly linked with the sacrament of
the Lord's Supper and Christ's words:
"I am the bread which came down from
heaven" (John 6, 41).   *RG*

Hugo van der Goes
(c. 1440–1482)

66 The Mourning of Christ,
c. 1480
Canvas, 53.5 x 38.5 cm
Acquired as a gift from O. Huldschinsky,
1900

This picture in tempera on canvas is one
of the few 15th-century paintings using
this technique to have survived. It shows
Christ's followers mourning his death.
In the foreground is the Mother of God,
crossing her hand over her breast and
inclining her lowered head slightly to the
side. Next to her is John, supporting her
and trying to comfort her. The group is
completed by Mary Magdalene and the
two other Marys. In the background the
hill of Golgotha and a narrow strip of
blue sky can be seen. The composition

and the event depicted are incomplete without the reference point for the lamentation and mourning. The former companion piece is a depiction of the dead Christ (New York, private collection). RG

Master of 1499 (active c. 1500)

67 The Annunciation to Mary (Diptych)
Oak, semicircular at the top,
each panel 15.9 x 9.5 cm
Acquired 1830

This anonymous master, a successor of Hugo van der Goes, was presumably active in Bruges and Ghent c. 1500. He owes his name to the diptych dated 1499 for Abbot Christian de Hondt in Antwerp. The scene shown on our diptych follows the Gospel of St. Luke (1, 16-38). It shows the Archangel Gabriel proclaiming the conception and birth of Christ to Mary.

The composition is treated entirely in the style of miniature painting, and is not an independent invention by the Master of 1499. It reflects, as scholars have acknowledged for some time, a lost work by Hugo van der Goes, dating from his later period and close to the Death of the Virgin Mary in Bruges, dating from c. 1480. RG

Geertgen tot Sint Jans
(1460/65 – after 1490)

68 John the Baptist in the Wilderness
c.1490
Oak, 42 x 28 cm
Acquired 1902

The painter lived and worked with the "Sint-Jans-Heren", the Knights of St. John of Jerusalem, in Haarlem, which accounts for his name. This panel, showing John the Baptist meditating in a lonely forest, was presumably intended as a devotional image for the Haarlem Knights of St. John. The saint, dressed in a brown camel-hair robe and a blue cloak, sits on a grassy rock ledge with his head leaning thoughtfully on his hand. He is meditating about Christ's imminent sufferings and the grace of the forgiveness of sins. Thistle and columbine at his feet are symbolic references to Christ's Passion. The lamb is resting at John's side. It is his attribute, and a symbol of Christ, whom John himself called "the Lamb of God who takes away the sins of the world". RG

Master of the Virgo inter Virgines
(active 1470–1500)

69 The Adoration of the Kings
c. 1485
Oak, 63 x 48 cm
Acquired as a gift from Jacques Seligmann, Paris, 1910

This anonymous master was active from 1470 to 1500 in Delft and presumably also in Gouda. The influence of Justus van Gent and Hugo van der Goes suggests that he probably spent a short time in the southern Netherlands. The Virgo Master, with Geertgen tot Sint Jans, is one of the most important and strikingly individual artists of his time in the northern Netherlands. *The Adoration of the Kings* is a typical work by this master, distinguished by its delicate, finely balanced colouring and lively use of line. The figures are unmistakable: apparently fragile, with dainty, somewhat theatrical gestures. The design of the faces is highly individual. They look ill and exhausted, with sunken cheeks, high foreheads and receding hair. The inner tension of profound religious feeling seems to have seized the figures and made its mark on their outward appearance.   *RG*

Hans Memling (c. 1434–1494)

70 Mary Enthroned with the Child
c. 1485
Oak, 66 x 46.5 cm
Acquired with the A. Thiem Collection, Berlin/San Remo Collection, 1904

Mary is seated on a Renaissance throne made of white stone, holding the naked child on her lap with both hands. An angel has appeared from the left, and is offering the child a red carnation. The flower is a symbolic reference to the Passion that lies ahead of Christ. On a bench to Mary's right is a brass jug filled with columbine, irises and white lilies. The white lily symbolises Mary's purity. The columbine and iris were perceived as attributes of the Queen of Heaven, but also as symbols of the spiritual pain that Mary was to suffer during Christ's Passion. This pictorial type, with the child sitting on the Madonna's left-hand side, was much varied by Memling. The composition goes back originally to a model by Rogier van der Weyden, which has survived in the form of a silver-pencil drawing in Rotterdam.   *RG*

Hans Memling (c. 1434–1494)

71 Mary with the Child, 1487
Oak, 41.5 x 31.5 cm
Acquired 1862

Mary is sitting in front of a stone parapet. The graceful quality of the scene is
expressed in the delicate gesture with
which Mary is offering the child an
apple. From the early Middle Ages the
apple was perceived as the forbidden
fruit from the tree of knowledge, which
Eve picked and gave to Adam. This
alludes to the old antithesis of Eve and
Mary. Offering the apple further symbolised that Christ took the sins of the
world upon himself in order to redeem
mankind. This Madonna must have been
painted for the Florentine merchant
Benedetto Portinari (1466–1551), who
lived in Bruges, as the central panel of a
small triptych. The portrait of Portinari
and the image of his patron saint, Benedict, which once framed this Madonna
panel, were in the infirmary of Santa
Maria Nuova in Florence until 1824.
They are now in the Uffizi. *RG*

Master of the Joseph Sequence
(active c. 1490–1500)

72 Joseph is Sold by His Brothers;
Joseph is Appointed Governor by
Potiphar
Oak, circular, each diameter 153 cm
Acquired 1889

It seems likely that the anonymous
master was active in Brussels, probably
c. 1490 to 1500. Stylistically he is a distant successor of Rogier van der Weyden.
According to the provenance of an altar
in Brussels he was also known earlier as
the "Master of the Afflighem Abbey".
His name derives from six large-format
circular pictures showing scenes from
the story of Joseph in Egypt, of which
four are in Berlin and one each in
Munich (Alte Pinakothek) and New
York (The Metropolitan Museum of
Art). Joseph was thrown into a pit by his
brothers, who sold him to Egypt, where
he achieved high honours at Pharaoh's
court after many trials, and was seen as a
paragon of honesty and virtue in the late
Middle Ages. *RG*

Juan de Flandes
(documented from 1496–1519)

73 Christ Appears to Mary
c. 1500/04
Oak, 21.6 x 16 cm
Acquired 1929

This artist's real name remains unknown.
However, the name by which he is
generally known suggests that he came
from Flanders. He was mentioned as
court painter to Queen Isabella the
Catholic of Castile from 1496 until she
died in 1504. This small panel shows
Mary kneeling at a prie-dieu in an open
pillared hall. She is turning to her son,
whom she believed dead, who has appeared to her and is showing her the
stigmata of his Passion. The painting
was originally part of a sequence of 47
small panels, all roughly the same size,
with scenes from the lives of Christ and
Mary. They were painted between 1496
and 1504 for Queen Isabella of Castile,
but only 28 are still in existence. Juan de
Flandes was responsible for most of them,
and either painted them personally or
with assistance from his studio. Three of
the pictures can be attributed to Michel
Sittow (c. 1469–1525). *RG*

Hieronymus Bosch (c. 1450–1516)

74 John on Patmos, c. 1505
Oak, 63 x 43.3 cm
Acquired 1907

Bosch treated the customary subjects,
scenes from the life and passion of Christ,
very powerfully but in direct dependence
on the iconographic tradition. But here
too we come across an aspect that had
not existed before in this form. The earth
is populated with demons put together
from human, animal and inanimate parts,
but capable of living, despite all their
distance from real life. In these surroundings the saints appear, withdrawn and
tolerant, quiet and steadfast. John the
Apostle, the author of Revelation, sits on
a hilltop with book and pen, looking out
over open countryside with a river. The
angel standing on the hill shows him
the divine apparition of the woman of
the apocalypse, whom the Middle Ages
recognised as the Mother of God. *RG*

Michel Sittow   (c. 1469–1525/26)

75   Mary with the Child,
c. 1515/18
Oak, 32 x 24.5 cm
Acquired 1914. Property of the
Kaiser Friedrich-Museums-Verein

Sitto came from Reval. He settled in
Bruges in 1484, and was trained there by
Hans Memling. He became court painter
to Queen Isabella the Catholic of Castile
in Toledo in 1492. He returned to the
Netherlands in 1502, but was back in
Reval from 1506. In 1514 he travelled
to the court of King Christian II of
Denmark in Copenhagen, and worked
in Mechlin for the regent Margaret of
Austria in the following year.

Another journey took him to Vallado-
lid, before he went back to the Netherlands again in 1516, where he entered
into the service of the later Emperor
Charles V. In 1518 he finally settled in
his home town, where he died in high
esteem.

One of Sittow's most beautiful and
typical pictures is his *Mary with the Child*.
This Madonna panel was originally the
left-hand wing of a diptych. The right-
hand wing is now in Washington D.C.
(National Gallery of Art). It shows the
donor Don Diego de Guevara (d. 1520),
chancellor to Margaret of Austria and
Knight of the Order of Calatrava.   RG

Gerard David   (c. 1460–1523)

76   Christ on the Cross, c. 1515
Oak, semicircular at the top, 141 x 100 cm
Acquired with the Solly Collection, 1821

Gerard David was born in the Dutch
city of Oudewater. In 1484 he moved to
Brugge where, with a few interruptions,
he lived and worked until his death.
David's work forms a link between the
15th-century Netherlandish masters and
the new line taken in the Renaissance.
His works have a quiet monumental quality and a clear arrangement of
figures, who relate in an innovative
way to the space that surrounds them
In this respect David's work represents a
crucial stage on the way towards uniform
painterly control over the pictorial
space.

This scene of *Christ on the Cross* dates
from the artist's late period. The colouring, dominated by notes of green and
blue, is strangely cool and reticent, although extremely refined in its nuanced
gradations. The events of the picture are
portrayed both succinctly and plainly,
corresponding with the consistently uniform colouring, which creates a strongly
atmospheric effect.   RG

Jean Bellegambe
(c. 1468/70 – after 1534)

77 Triptych with the Last Judgement,
c. 1520/25
Oak, arched top, central panel
222 x 178 cm,
each wing 222 x 82 cm
Acquired with the Solly Collection,
1821

Christ is enthroned on the rainbow, with
the globe at his feet. The sword and lily
emerging from his mouth are symbols of
justice and grace. The graves from which
the dead are rising open at the sound of
the trumpets. Bright light and surging
darkness are spreading from the centre
to the sides. On the right at the front,
the godless are driven into hell by the
archangel, and there receive just punishment for their mortal sins. The vision of
paradise on the left, the New Jerusalem,
forms a contrast with the torments of
hell. Here the blessed are rewarded for
the mercy they have practised on earth,
so that finally they can climb upwards to
God.   *RG*

Quinten Massys   (1465/66–1530)

78 Madonna Enthroned, c. 1520
Oak, semicircular curved top, 135 x 90 cm
Acquired 1823

The well and fenced garden in the background allude to Mary's virginity; the
apple symbolises original sin, purged
by Christ. Bread and wine refer to the
sacrament of the Lord's Supper. The
influence of the Italian Renaissance,
above all the work of Leonardo da Vinci,
combines with the detailed realism of
Netherlandish art in a unique way here.
The picture was formerly in the possession of Archduchess Isabella Clara
Eugenia (1566–1633), the daughter of
Philip II of Spain.   *RG*

Antwerp Master, c. 1520

79 The Beheading of John
the Baptist
Oak, 48 x 35 cm
Acquired 1906

St. Matthew's Gospel (14, 3-12) tells us
that Herod had John the Baptist beheaded because John had publicly reproached
him for his adulterous relationship with
Herodias, the wife of his brother Philip.
In the background, Salome is dancing for
Herod in the hall of the palace, so that
she will be able to ask for John's death, at
her mother Herodias's behest. The dead
man is lying in the foreground, and the
executioner has seized his head to give it
to Salome.   RG

Joos van Cleve   (c. 1480/85–1540)

80 Triptych with the Adoration of the
Kings, c. 1520
Oak, central panel 72 x 52 cm,
each wing 69 x 22 cm
Acquired 1843

Joos van Cleve, who was from the Lower
Rhine, was crucially influenced by Hans
Memling and Gerard David in Bruges.
In Antwerp he addressed the work of
Patenier, Massys and the "Antwerp Man-
nerists". He must have encountered
Leonardo da Vinci's work on a visit to
Italy. This small triptych dates from his
middle period. The central panel shows
the Adoration of the Kings, framed by
the wings depicting SS. Catherine and
Barbara.   RG

Joachim Patenier (c. 1480–1524)

81 Rest on the Flight to Egypt c. 1520
Oak, 62 x 78 cm
Acquired with the Solly Collection, 1821

Patenier worked in Antwerp as an
independent master from 1515, and
there in 1520/21 he met Albrecht Dürer,
who mentioned him in his travel jour-
nal as a "good landscape painter", thus
using this term for the first time. His
panoramic landscapes, whose ornate
details combine to form a cosmic view
of nature, considerably influenced Pieter
Bruegel the Elder. Patenier introduced
events drawn from the apocryphal
gospels' accounts of the Holy Family's
flight into his landscapes. These include
idols falling from their plinths and the
legend of the miraculous harvest. This is
the story of corn that ripened overnight,
deceiving Herod's soldiers, who broke off
their pursuit of the Holy Family.   *RG*

Lucas van Leyden (c. 1489–1533)

82 The Game of Chess, c. 1508
Oak, 27 x 35 cm
Acquired with the Suermondt Collection,
1874

The game between a young woman and
a man is central to this image. A few
spectators are following their moves with
lively interest.

The chessboard has twelve by eight
squares. This is the Courier version, a
special form of the modern game of
chess, in which each player had four ad-
ditional pawns, and four new pieces, two
"couriers", an "adviser" and a "straggler".
The game was seen as a metaphor of

love and the game of love; the result of the contest is not so important, since the loser will be lucky in love. *The Game of Chess* is one of the first examples of Dutch genre painting.   RG

Lucas van Leyden   (c. 1489–1533)

83   Mary with the Child and Angels
c. 1520
Oak, semicircular at the top, 74 x 44 cm
Acquired 1892

Carel van Mander tells us in his *Schilder-Boeck* (1604) that Lucas van Leyden "produced very handsome and finely executed copperplate engravings of his own invention" even as a child of nine. He met Dürer in Antwerp in 1521. He worked as a painter and copperplate engraver, produced woodcuts and drew designs for stained glass. He left behind a copious graphic oeuvre of far-reaching significance. Our picture tackles a traditional motif, which the artist placed against a background of fantastic Renaissance architecture. The Christ Child is surrounded by angels playing musical instruments. Apple, carnation and grape

are Symbols of original sin purged by Christ and also refer to the passion and the work of redemption.   RG

Jan Gossaert   (c. 1478–1532)

84   Christ on the Mount of Olives
c.1509/10
Oak, 85 x 63 cm
Acquired 1848

The gospels tell us how Christ, who went to the Mount of Olives with his disciples at night after the Last Supper, knelt down and prayed: "Father, if it is your will, take this cup from me, yet not my will but yours be done." An angel then appeared to him from heaven to strengthen him. In his anguish he prayed with all the greater intensity, and his sweat became like drops of blood falling to the ground. Then he rose from prayer and came to his disciples, only to find them asleep, exhausted with grief (Luke 22. 42–45). After this, Judas appeared at the head of the pursuers in the Garden of Gethsemane, went up to Christ and greeted him with the traitor's kiss. This picture is one of the first night scenes. The effective handling of light reinforces the drama of the events.   RG

Jan Gossaert (c. 1478–1532)

85 Neptune and Amphitrite, 1516
Oak, 188 x 124 cm
Acquired with the Solly Collection, 1821

Neptune and Amphitrite are standing on
a low plinth surrounded by water in a
domed structure supported by columns.
We are looking into the mighty sea-
god's shrine, in which he appears to us
with his spouse in statuesque symmetry,
but with a sense of being a living physical presence. On the plinth is the artist's
proud signature "IOANNES MAL-
BODIVS PINGEBAT", dated 1516.
Top right are the device and name of the
patron, Philip of Burgundy (1464–1524).
This large picture was part of a lavish
decoration that Philip had commissioned
for his castle. Gossaert had accompanied
his patron to Rome in 1508, where he
drew ancient buildings and sculptures for
him. This was one of the earliest Italian
journeys undertaken by Netherlandish
artists, which led them to address and
come to terms with Italian art. This impressive composition is inspired by these
travels and impressions, and also by ideas
derived from Albrecht Dürer and Jacopo
de' Barbari.   *RG*

Jan Gossaert (c. 1478–1532)

86 The Fall of Man, c. 1515
Oak, 170 x 114 cm
Acquired 1830

Gossaert was particularly fascinated by
depicting the first man and woman.
No other pictorial theme occurs more
frequently in his paintings and drawings. This picture shows Adam and Eve
between the tree of life and the tree of
knowledge. Eve has been seduced by the
serpent, and is offering Adam an apple.
A monkey with a pear it has bitten into
is crouching at Adam's feet. This animal
was considered a symbol of man's animal desires and sin in general from time
immemorial. The owl, as the night-bird,
was seen as a symbol of evil and lack of
chastity. In the background is the Garden
of Eden, with numerous minor scenes
to place the events in the foreground
in their proper context. The fountain of
life and the creation of Eve are shown in
the centre; on the left is God's warning
not to touch the tree of knowledge, and
following this the expulsion from paradise and Cain killing his brother
Abel.   *RG*

the curse that Eve brought upon mankind. In the moulding is the inscription: "VERVS DEVS ET HOMO—CASTA MATER ET VIRGO" (A True God and Man, a Pure Mother and Virgin). *RG*

Jan Gossaert   (c. 1478–1532)

87   Mary with the Child, c. 1530
Oak, 44.7 cm x 38.2 cm
Acquired with the Solly Collection, 1821

The reddish-brown rear section of a trompe l'œil frame forms the background of this picture, and Mary's beautiful face stands out from it in lavish contrast. Mary is holding a grape in her raised hand, while the child is touching an apple. The apple, which once sealed the fall of man, here becomes a symbol of the hope of redemption. The grape is a sign that Christ's blood will wipe out

Brunswick Monogrammist
(active 2nd quarter of the 16th century)

88   The Loose Society, c. 1535/40
Oak, 29 x 45 cm
Acquired 1832

The scene is about abandoned behaviour by young men and women in a brothel. The scribbles on the walls and the birdcage hanging on the door are unmistakable signs that this is a house of ill repute. The subject derives from the thought pattern that was most powerfully expressed in the parable of the Prodigal Son (Luke 15, 11-32). This painting, which is one of the best of its kind, is usually attributed to the "Brunswick Monogrammist", who specialised in biblical scenes with many figures and "loose societies", and who was earlier identified with Jan van Amstel, or rather Jan Sanders van Hemessen. *RG*

Jan van Scorel (1495–1562)

89 Portrait of a Man, c. 1530
Oak, semicircular at the top,
65 x 44 cm
Acquired 1907. Property of the
Kaiser Friedrich-Museums-Verein

This portrait was originally the left-hand
half of a diptych. Its companion-piece,
a portrayal of *The Mother of God with
Child*, is now in the Kartinnaia Gallery
of Tambov in Russia. The background is
a summer landscape with bizarre rocks
and ancient ruins, which Scorel had been
able to study during his stay in Italy.
The artist has been appointed inspector
of the papal antique collection in the
Belvedere by Pope Hadrian VI in 1522,
an office previously held by no less than
Raphael.   *RG*

Anthonis Mor (1516/20–1575/76)

90 Portrait of Two Canons, 1544
Oak, 74 x 96 cm
Acquired 1859

This double portrait of the Utrecht
canons is the earliest dated work by
Anthonis Mor. The subjects here are the
Utrecht canons Cornelis van Horn and
Anthonis Taets van Anleronghen, who
had both undertaken pilgrimages to the
Holy Land and to Jerusalem. Anthonis
Taets had also been to Rome, Santiago
de Compostella and various other places
that have never been individually identified. Van Horn's journey is said to date
from 1520, in other words it took place
well before the time the portrait, which
was intended to keep its memory alive,
was painted. The devoutly folded hands,
the palm fronds on their shoulders and
the inscription are evidence of the pious
hope of gaining salvation for their souls
and eternal peace from the pilgrimage.
Anthonis Mor's double portrait identifies
an important phase in the development
of the Dutch group portrait, which was
to reach its apogee in the 17th century
in the portraits of regents and archers by
Frans Hals and Rembrandt.   *RG*

Pieter Bruegel the Elder
(1525/30–1569)

91 Two Chained Monkeys, 1562
Oak, 20 x 23 cm
Acquired 1931

The picture shows two monkeys chained
to an iron ring and sitting in a vaulted

window opening. The two animals have obviously come to terms with their sad fate. One is crouching on the floor, with his back bent and huddling in on himself, staring into space, while the other is looking at the viewer. Behind them is a view of an open landscape, flooded with bright daylight, and seen without transition, as though from a high look-out post. The city of Antwerp basks under a pale blue sky. The monkeys Bruegel has painted are of the genus ceropithecidae, collared mangabeys, which inhabit the west coast of Africa. However, Bruegel's picture is not an animal study but an allegory of captivity and the hope of a free life that is inherent in all creatures.

RG

Pieter Bruegel the Elder
(1525/30–1569)

92 The Dutch Proverbs, 1559
Oak, 117 x 163 cm
Acquired 1914

The picture brings together 100 proverbs and places them in surroundings that are as real as the people's behaviour, revealed in terse and apposite form by the wise sayings. The individual scenes are played out side by side, without being directly dependent on each other. A village near the sea provides a spacious stage for the apparently everyday tasks of its inhabitants. The background for all the varied activity is made up of a farmhouse, dilapidated huts, a stone bridge with pillory and tower, the village square at the centre of the activity and a farmstead among cornfields near the wood. In the distance is the open sea, shining in the sun of a late summer's day. The painting's old title, *The Upside-Down World*, derives from the symbol of a globe standing on its head. This is intended to illustrate that we are in a world in which nothing is as it should be. The wise sayings are evidence of man's folly and sinfulness in a crazy world that has turned away from God. This proverb picture is evidence of Bruegel's intense pre-occupation with the spiritual and moral questions of his time, which give the work its timeless validity

RG

Maerten van Heemskerck
(1498–1574)

93 Momos Reproaches the Works of
the Gods, 1561
Oak, 120 x 174 cm
Acquired from the Royal Palaces

The Olympian gods have assembled on a
flowery meadow in a park-like landscape
full of antique monuments, in order to
present the works of art that they have
created. We can see Neptune with the
horse that he has created, Vulcan with the
virgin he has made and Minerva with
her impressive palace that towers up in
the background. Momos is the judge
of the gods' competition, the winged
personification of fault-finding, who
criticises everything indiscriminately.
Momos requires that men's chests be
opened, so that everyone can see into
their hearts. The little sculpture on his
arm underlines how foolish and arrogant
his request is. This learned scene with a
Humanist slant goes back to the ancient
poet Lucian.   *RG*

Pieter Aertsen   (1508–1575)

94 Market Woman at the Vegetable
Stall, 1567
Oak, 111 x 110 cm
Acquired 1961

A young peasant woman is standing
amidst the almost oppressive abundance
of fruit for kitchen and table, pointing
invitingly to her wares with outspread
arms. The goods on offer include cu-
cumbers, pumpkins, turnips, radishes,
white, red and Savoy cabbage, apples,
peaches, walnuts and sweet chestnuts.
Waffles, bread, cakes and pastries are
mingled with them. Aertsen's still lifes
often refer antithetically to man's dependence on nature and slavery to the senses.
The lovers embracing in the background
on the right are intended as a warning
that giving in to the senses, the "voluptas
carnis", is a threat to man's salvation.   *RG*

Paulus Bril (1554–1626)

95 Mountainous Seashore, c. 1624
Canvas, 58.3 x 87 cm
Acquired 1821

This is not a real place, but an idealistic
landscape typical of its period, bringing
together the sea, magnificent mountain
forms, cave-like gloom and blazing light.
Skilfully distributed examples of busy,
maritime activity make this an artful
composition. This picture is considered
to be one of Bril's very best, very late
works. He travelled to Rome in 1574,
where was influenced by the work of
Adam Elsheimer and Annibale Carracci's
landscapes. *IG*

Peter Paul Rubens (1577–1640)

96 Christ Hands Peter the Keys of
Heaven, c. 1614
Oak, 182.6 x 159 cm
Acquired 1936

This monumental composition illustrates
St. Matthew's Gospel (16, 18), according to which Christ chose the fisherman
Simon of Galilee with the words "You
are Peter, and on this rock I will build
my church ...". The handing over of the
keys is also to be read as a reference to
the establishment of the papacy. Rubens
painted the picture for the tomb of
Pieter Bruegel the Elder in the Kapelle-
kerck in Brussels. *IG*

Peter Paul Rubens (1577–1640)

97 St. Sebastian, c. 1618
Canvas, 200 x 128 cm
Acquired 1878

This is presumably the "Sebastian" that
Rubens offered to sell to an English-
man in 1618 as the "finest flower of his
work". At that time he also re-worked
the somewhat older picture. The larger-
than-life figure of the martyr is reminiscent of classical ancient art, and the work
of Mantegna and Titian. *MW*

Peter Paul Rubens (1577–1640)

98   Perseus Freeing Andromeda
c. 1620/22
Oak, 100 x 138.5 cm
Acquired from the Royal Palaces, 1830

Rubens presented the Andromeda
myth, derived from Ovid's account in
the *Metamorphoses*, with some narrative
breadth. Andromeda was chained to a
rock and exposed to a sea-monster as a
punishment for her mother's arrogance,
who had dared to boast that she and her
daughter were more beautiful than the
Nereids. Perseus, who had just returned
from his victorious struggle with the
feared Gorgon Medusa, is hurrying on
to the scene to free Andromeda from
her chains; the slain monster is lying
on the left. The light-toned, softly and
atmospherically shaded colour is typical of Rubens's work in the 1620s. As a
painter trained in the humanities he was
able to appropriate from antiquity: the
form of Andromeda and of the putto
who is working on her chains is based
on the Roman statue of *Venus felix*.   CB

Jan Fyt (1611–1661)

99   Dogs with Shot Game, 1649
Canvas 138.3 x 198.5 cm
Acquired 1874

Presumably intended as a fireplace
piece, this Flemish masterpiece depicting a hunting still life shows the end of
a successful hunt in a landscape bathed
in evening light. On the right the eye is
carried into the reddish-coloured distance under grey clouds, and there are
other spots of intense red in the wounds
of the deer's body and on the hunting
bag. In terms of colour and brushstrokes,
the lifelessness of the prey with the
grey-blue plumage of the partridges, in
which the yellowish-brown coat is finely
differentiated, forms a contrast with the
compulsive agility of the spotted hounds.
This polarity of passivity and activity
gives the work the Baroque drama of a
historical painting.   IG

Peter Paul Rubens (1577–1640)

100 Child with Bird, c. 1624/25
Oak, 50.8 x 40.5 cm
Acquired from the Royal Palaces

Rubens had a considerable reputation as a portrait artist, but was never officially commissioned to paint children. Thus he painted his own children, or children from the family circle. The child depicted here has recently been identified as the artist's nephew Philip, born in 1611, the son of his brother who died at an early age. The work beautifully captures the intuitive nature of children. Rubens's portraits of children usually do more than simply present individual characters. He always saw them as angels or putti, and he often presented them as such in mythological or religious paintings. The linked motifs of child and bird could be explained simply by the desire to enliven the composition, but it could also have a moral significance, alluding to the notion of the tamed bird and man's susceptibility to Christian education.   *CB*

Peter Paul Rubens (1577–1640)

101 The Duck Hunters, c. 1635/38
Oak, 113 x 176 cm
Acquired 1927

This late Rubens panorama thrives on contrast: rain is juxtaposed with reddish-gold evening light, which is again broken by the artfully arranged copes. The light is conveyed by thick paint applied to the gnarled trunks, and the wood acquires its depth from this and the clearings.

One of the modifications made to the painting during its execution was the addition of the hunters, who were painted on a separate panel and then attached. This altered the bucolic scene of the maidens with their cows, a topos on which Rubens had relied for two decades.   *MW*

Joos de Momper (1564–1635)

102   Landscape with Grottoes and
John the Baptist
Oak, 105.3 x 73.4 cm
Acquired 1962

Within the oeuvre of the Flemish
landscape painter Joos de Momper, the
"grotto" theme is an extremely popular
one, which was multi-faceted and often
included Alpine motifs. The Berlin picture dates from the late 1620s and is one
of the rare vertical formats. It presents
a scene in close-up, embedded in natural rock formations and enlivened by a
waterfall and romantic trees. The solitude,
created by nature, shady and mysterious, in which John the Baptist sits by
a spring with the lamb, drawing water
with a baptismal cup, seems to draw in
the viewer as a quiet and intimate friend.
His only view of the world of men is
afforded to him as if through a window
in the picture. Through the rocky gate he
can see a distant landscape with a castle,
vaulted by light and a high sky. The composition draws a wonderful tension from
this contrast of distance and proximity
gloom in the foreground and brightness
in the background.   *IG*

Peter Paul Rubens (1577–1640)

103   St. Cecilia, c. 1639/40
Oak, 177 x 139 cm
Acquired from the Royal Palaces,
1830

Cecilia, the patron saint of music, is sitting at a virginals and looking upwards,
her mouth open in ecstasy so that she
can listen to the heavenly sounds. At the
time of the Counter-Reformation Cecilia was considered the embodiment of
ecstasy induced by divine music, which
was evidence of the existence of God.
The monumental column symbolises her
steadfast belief.

Rubens used virtuoso painterly effects to design the meeting of the divine
and the earthly in such a way that the
viewer could "believe" the ecstasy. The
colour values, dominated by the second-
ary triad of green-orange-violet, are
mutually enhancing. The colour seems to
detach itself from the material world and
make itself independent. The diversity
of colour is reminiscent of the common
Baroque principle of synaesthesia. Numerous theories were developed to relate
colour combinations to musical chords,
and it is well known that Rubens took
an interest in colour theory.   *CB*

David Ryckaert the Younger
(1612–1661)

104   The Village Idiot
Oak, 33.3 x 25.5 cm
Acquired 1874

Ryckaert works in the thematic and
painterly tradition of Brouwer. He always
shows an almost loving sense of observation that goes well beyond the rapid
imposition of type or the caricature of
popular figures that is typical in bucolic
subjects. These three boys are not just
an interesting study of movement, but
the figure in the centre is a graceful and
sensitive portrait of a child. Traditionally
the figures are fitted into a story: thus the
main figure is the village idiot, who is
being mocked by the boy in the centre,
an apprentice. The third lad seems to
be passing water against the wall of the
building on the left.   IG

Adriaen Brouwer   (1605/06–1638)

105   Dune Landscape with
Moonlight
Oak 25.8 x 34.8 cm
Acquired 1874

This simple landscape with sandy dunes,
windswept shrubs and bushes, and a
distant view of the sea conveys an
astonishing sense of spatial depth and
mood. The key feature is the blazing
moonlight, which enlivens the landscape
details. Brouwer's painting technique
is loose and broad, and paint is applied
alternately thickly or thinly. He did not
paint landscapes until his late period. The
Berlin picture is generally considered to
be his finest work in this genre.   IG

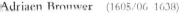

Frans Snyders (1579–1657)

106 Still Life with Lobster and Fruit
Canvas, 91.1 x 122.6 cm
Acquired 1904

The eye is caught by the gleaming red
of a lobster lying on a Chinese porcelain
plate. Set down under this is a blackish-
blue capercaillie; under it the yellowish
body of a plucked chicken. This apparently random accumulation of objects
reveals a tension-filled rhythm of composition and colour, and also a bravura
painterly grasp of material qualities. As
well as this, the special order of symbolic
messages is conveyed: the left-hand half
is dominated by earthly desires and in-
stincts, embodied above all by the cat.
In the right-hand field are grapes, wine
and strawberries, symbols of Christ and
paradise. Snyders was one of the most
vivacious inventors in Flemish still-life
painting, very diverse in his motifs, and
satisfied a very broad range of patrons
with his Baroque and generously painted
pictures.   IC

Jan Brueghel the Elder
(1568–1625)

107 Bouquet of Flowers, c. 1619/20
Oak, 64 x 59 cm
Acquired 1862

Jan Brueghel, who was also a versatile landscape and history painter, was responsible for numerous important floral still lifes. It was a popular theme, particularly as new exotic flowers were increasingly being imported from the new world. Brueghel was painter to the Archdukes Albrecht and Isabella, and was able to study rare flowers in their gardens in Brussels, which he then rendered very precisely and at their most beautiful stage of development. Brueghel brings flowers which bloom at different times together in one bouquet, so it must have taken several months for these early pictures to be completed. For later versions he was able to draw on existing individual studies.   CB

Anton van Dyck (1599–1641)

108   Portrait of a Genoese Gentleman;
Portrait of a Genoese Lady
Canvas, 203 x 117.3; 203 x 118.3 cm
Acquired 1901

New evidence suggests that the first-known owner of both portraits, the important collector Costantino Balbi, did not acquire the female portrait until 1724, but had acquired the supposed companion-portrait from the estate of Bartolomeo Saluzzo as early as 1706. The gentleman was formerly thought to be Bartolomeo Giustiniani, and the picture may indeed have come from this family. There is also the matter of the formal and artistic differences: the gentleman fills the width of the picture more completely, and is sitting lower. Here the carpet is missing, there the landscape view. The architectural forms also differ in detail. But above all the brushstrokes in the male portrait are broader, the paint thicker, while in the female portrait the surfaces are smoother and more delicately handled, with small highlights and finely-drawn detail in the eyes and mouth. This different handling of paint can also be seen in the gown, most clearly in the lace. Van Dyck probably spent almost six years in Italy from late 1621, particularly in Genoa.   MW

Simon de Vos   (1603–1676)

109   The Castigation of Cupid
Oak, 54 x 80 cm
Acquired 1829

De Vos presents an incident that is not usually mentioned in literature about Cupid, with verve and brilliant colour. It takes place in a lavishly decorated Renaissance hall. An elegantly dressed gentleman is whipping the boy Cupid, who is curling up in shame, before the eyes of Venus. She is trying to come to her son's aid, but is prevented by a helmeted warrior, who could be Mars. Terrified women are throwing their musical instruments on the ground. A group of little cupids is running to find a way out. An older women is maliciously showing the viewer an empty purse. This is, of course, the reason for the annoyance of the cavalier who is punishing the god of love.   IG

Jacob Jordaens   (1593–1678)

110   The Abduction of Europa
1615/16
Canvas 173 x 235 cm
Acquired 1981

Jupiter, the father of the gods, was attracted to Europa, the beautiful daughter of the King of Phoenicia, and played a deceitful trick to abduct her, by transforming himself into a bull. Jordaens presented this story from Ovid's *Metamorphoses* as a lively festive scene. Blossoms, gleaming fabrics and flowing blond hair embellish the rosy nakedness of the women. Europa, clearly based on Rubens's model, is enthroned on the bull, and is crowned with flowers. The colouring of this early work by Jordaens is bright and glowing; he painted it shortly after attaining the rank of master.   IG

Jacob Jordaens (1593–1678)

111   Christ Appears to the Three
Marys as a Gardener, c. 1616
Oak, 107 x 90.5 cm
Acquired 1928

The women, who had come out to tend
Christ's grave, are the first to experience
the miracle of his resurrection. According to St. Matthew's Gospel (28, 1-10),
he gave them a message for the disciples.
But the composition is determined
by the idea of "Noli me tangere" (Do
not touch me), which comes from St.
John's Gospel (20, 14-18), where Mary
Magdalene first of all took Christ for
the gardener. The lively movement, the
structured sense of composition, vigor-
ous brushstrokes and glowing colour give
this early work the Baroque excitement
that is typical of the great Flemish artists.

IG

bit of criticism. While music was considered to be a liberal art, painting was seen
as a "lowly" craft. By representing himself
as a musician, Teniers was consciously appealing for a revaluation of the painter's
social status.

CB

David Teniers the Younger
(1610–1690)

112   The Painter with his Family
c. 1645/46
Oak, 38 x 58 cm
Acquired from the Royal Palaces,
1829

Teniers, who is playing the viola da
gamba, his wife and their son have come
to the terrace to play music. The two
people on the left of the picture must
also be members of the family. By type,
the painting is in the tradition of Flemish
bourgeois family portraits. Making music
together was seen as the epitome of family harmony, but here it could also be a

Cornelis de Vos (1585–1651)

113   Magdalena and Jan Baptist de Vos,
c. 1621/??
Canvas, 78 x 92 cm
Acquired 1837

De Vos established himself as a specialist
in family portraits, which often reveal
the influence of Anton van Dyck. His
characterisation of his own children
shows how well he knew them as a
father, and their rich clothing shows a
bourgeois desire to express social status.

CB

give way to a sumptuous, magnificently coloured presentation.

The Berlin picture can be classed as "showpiece still life". Three heavy garlands with strands of ivy winding through them are arranged in a complex, decorative and symmetrical fashion around a stone. The artful combination of pieces of fruit, flowers and kinds of cereal at various stages of development is enhanced by the notion of vanity and an infusion of Christian meaning.   *IG*

Gonzales Coques, attributed to
(1614–1684)

115   Portrait of a Married Couple in the Park
Canvas, 239 x 174 cm
Acquired 1829

This portrait was long thought to be a Dutch work. More recently the seemingly Flemish, relaxed and generous painting style had been thought to show the stylistic qualities of the Antwerp genre and portrait painter Gonzales Coques. The figures are presented very prestigiously. They have so far not been identified, but their clothes and the grand atmosphere of the surrounding park suggest that they are members of Antwerp high society. Nevertheless the painter is able to replace refined social distance with individual and natural behaviour and gestures, and lively characterisation of the faces. Symbols of faith and love suggest that this is a portrait for a wedding or an engagement.   *IG*

Jan Davidsz de Heem
(1606–1683/84)

114   Cartouche of Fruit and Flowers with Wineglass, 1651
Canvas, 122.5 x 86.5 cm
Acquired 1878

De Heem was born in Utrecht and moved to Antwerp in 1636. Here his artistic approach moved closer to Flemish Baroque. Plainness and simplicity

Joachim Anthonisz Wtewael
(1566–1638)

116   Kitchen Piece with the Parable of the Great Feast, 1605
Canvas, 65 x 98 cm
Acquired 1927

The Gospels of St. Matthew and St. Luke contain accounts of the actions of a rich Pharisee as a parable of justice on Judgement Day. After many invited guests had

refused to attend his feast, he invited cripples and beggars from the street to eat and drink in his house. Wtewael uses a Mannerist approach and shifts the lively throng of poor people, surging out of town squares and appearing at the laid table, into a room in the background. Attention is principally paid to the kitchen in the foreground, which opens up like a stage. Here servants are working among a lavish display of vegetables, fish, game and kitchen equipment. Every action, every accidentally assembled still life embodies a popular allegory, usually of an erotic nature. Wtewael works with a bright, almost gaudy palette and a strong sense of painterly atmosphere. Late-Mannerist Italian and French influence can be seen in the bravura of his colour and technique.   *IG*

or semi-nude female figures. The composition depicts the events related in the Old Testament (II Samuel, 11-12), when King David watch the beautiful Bathsheba, wife of Uriah, as she bathed and desired her. After the heroic death of Uriah, which David brought about, Bathsheba became David's wife and the mother of the later King Solomon. The figure of David, previously in the window of the building on the right, is no longer recognisable because this part of the painting has darkened considerably. Cornelis Cornelisz was one of the leading painters in Haarlem; in this picture he adheres to a classical, academic formal language with clear signs of Mannerism. The subject gave him an opportunity to portray different variations of the motif of the female nude.   *BL*

Cornelis Cornelisz van Haarlem
(1562–1638)

117   Bathsheba Bathing, 1617
Canvas, 102 x 130 cm
Acquired 1821 with the Solly
Collection

With the background of a garden, laid out with bowers and hedges according to the principles of the early 17th century, the painting shows five nude

Gerard van Honthorst
(1590–1656)

118 The Liberation of Peter
c. 1616/18
Canvas, 131 x 181 cm
Acquired 1815

In the year 1615, "… when Caravaggio's manner was general" (Mancini/Bellori), the young Honthorst, like many Dutch painters, went to Rome. He had been trained in Abraham Bloemaert's large studio in Utrecht, and had familiarised himself with the style of Florentine and Venetian Mannerism there. But he detached himself from Mannerism as current in his homeland under the influence of Italian Renaissance art. Large-scale form, composition, drawing and contrasting light and shade now became fundamental. Our picture is the earliest known commission executed by Honthorst in Rome. It was painted in 1616/18 for art connoisseur and collector Marchese Vincenzo Giustiniani, a promoter of modern admiration of Caravaggio. In this composition Honthorst reduced the account in the Acts of the Apostles (12, 6-7) simply to the words "Get up quickly", with which the angel asked the astonished prisoner Peter to leave the gaol from the door that had burst open. The warriors and prison guards are left out, as are the chains that were said to have fallen from the prisoner's hands. All the characteristics of Caravaggio's style come into play in the concentration on Peter and the angel, their violent physical and spiritual movement, which is effectively carried by the magnificent handling of light and shade, the powerful plasticity of the design and the warmth of the colouring. They give the scene a magical sense of drama. Honthorst's angel's gesture is clearly borrowed directly from Caravaggio's *Calling of St. Matthew* in the church of San Luigi Francesi in Rome. This early pictorial invention by Honthorst seems to have been generally hailed as a masterpiece, and thus recurs in numerous replicas and copies. A drawing in the Kupferstichkabinett in Dresden used to be seen as a preliminary drawing by the artist for the Berlin painting, but it is now attributed to Abraham Bloemaert. *IG*

Matteus Stom   (1600 – after 1641)

119   Christ on the Mount of Olives
Canvas, 152 x 199 cm
Acquired 1969

Detailed research in to Matteus Stom's work has been undertaken only in recent decades—as is the case with all the Northern European artists strongly influenced by Caravaggio. Stom was acknowledged to be more important than his Utrecht teacher Gerard van Honthorst, and as one of the most interesting exponents of Dutch painting influenced by Caravaggio. From about 1630 up until the time of his death, Stom worked exclusively in Rome and Naples. The Berlin picture also shows Michelangelo da Caravaggio's poignantly realistic figure-style, combined with a highly individual clear and intense approach to colour. It is presumably part of a passion sequence with several parts painted for S. Efrem Nuovo in Naples in about 1631. Stom logically reduces the story of the Mount of Olives, traditionally presented broadly in pictorial art, with subsidiary scenes, to two half-figures. The sleeping disciples and any detailed representation of the place are omitted. Only the group

of Judas and the soldiers on the right in the background, lit by the white, frayed light of a candle, indicates that the scene is taking place at night. At the same time the stylised, blatant features of this group also underline the threatening nature of the event. Christ is kneeling at a stone table, with his hands folded in fervent prayer, and turning to the angel, who is close to him both physically and spiritually. Christ's eyes are following the angel's sweeping, powerful gesture, pointing with both arms to indicate the goblet, mystically glowing in the sidelighting, on the left-hand edge of the picture. Contrasting light and shade have been powerfully developed in this nocturnal situation, with supernatural light striking the main figures from the left, and increasing the drama. The two wonderfully modelled heads, inclined towards each other, and their concentrated expressions form the spiritual centre of the picture, and also its precise formal centre, with the angel's wings spanning almost the entire width of the picture. The heads are plastic and expressive, and this quality and their actions and gestures are continued in the, poetic, painterly treatment of the heavy garments with their rich folds.   *IG*

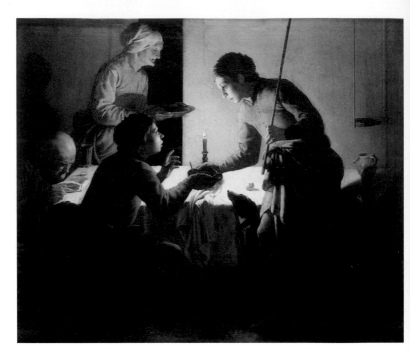

Hendrick ter Brugghen
(1588–1629)

120 Esau Sells his Birthright
Canvas, 84.9 x 116.3 cm
Acquired 1926

Hendrick ter Brugghen first studied under Abraham Bloemaert in Utrecht. After
that he spent the years 1604 to 1614 in
Italy, and was profoundly impressed by
the unique style of Michelangelo da Caravaggio. Art historians now consider him
to be one of the great masters of Utrecht
Caravaggism. This presentation of the
scene from Genesis (25, 29-34), in which
Esau returns hungry from hunting and
sells his birthright to his brother Jacob
for a dish of lentils, draws life entirely
from the expressive, silent dialogue between the brothers, staged only in terms
of movement. The fateful deal is concentrated on their hands, which are holding
the bowl of lentils. Directly above this
gesture, whitish-yellow candlelight forms
the centre of the picture, and illuminates
the beautifully formed profiles of the
boys, turned eloquently towards each
other.

But this is not all: the light also struc-
tures the space. The parents are present in
the room, apparently untouched by the
incident. The father is bending over the
table on the left-hand side and spooning
up his soup. Rebecca, the mother, busy
but restrained, is behind the table, carrying a copper plate, holding herself stiffly
with a positively dignified expression;
she casts a shadow on the rear wall. Individual objects form sparse still lifes.   *IG*

Abraham Bloemaert   (1564–1651)

121 Landscape with Farmstead,
Peasants and Tobias Setting Out with
the Angel, 1630
Canvas, 91.2 x 134.2 cm
Acquired 1927

Themes from the story of Tobias often
occur in 17th-century Dutch painting,
probably because of their moralising
content. The Berlin picture takes the
account in Tobias (5, 22 ff), in which
the young Tobias is sent out by his old,
blind father to raise a loan. Unknown to
Tobias, he is accompanied by the Arch-

angel Raphael as a protector. A striking feature of the Berlin composition is that the viewer sees the biblical motif far off in the background, almost as an unimportant staffage within a spacious landscape, rich in colour and atmosphere, under a big sky. The painter was most concerned with the decoratively drawn, detailed depiction of a run-down and yet lively farmstead, and also a group of figures in the foreground. Peasants in ragged clothes are sleeping or chatting by a rotten tree. The Tobias theme is taken up again here in the hand over the closed eyes of the recumbent old man and in the items suggesting a journey on foot. Bloemaert, who was a highly influential master in Utrecht, returned to this theme more than once.   IG

height and breadth of the picture, fringe a slightly upward-sloping path leading into an uncertain distance. The path is enlivened by alternate patterns of light and shade, in which tiny staffage figures can be discerned. The left-hand half of the picture opens up into an open plain, sketched in picturesque fashion. In contrast to the greenish-brown tunnel of trees, the meadow is depicted in light, bluish-green shades. At the foot of the path in the centre of the picture, the prophet Elijah meets an elderly widow and her son; the woman is handing the last of her food over to him. For this charitable sacrifice she will experience the miracle that her supplies will never run out, despite a drought in the land (1 Kings 17, 10).   IG

Jacob Jacobsz van Geel
(1584/85 – after 1638)

122 Wooded Landscape with Elijah and Zarpath's Widow, c. 1638
Canvas, 81 x 103 cm
Acquired 1927. Property of the Kaiser Friedrich-Museums-Verein

Mighty deciduous trees with gnarled, crooked trunks and roots, their branches fanning out heavily to span the whole

Willem Pietersz Buytewech
(1591/92–1624)

123   Interior with Cheerful Company,
c.1622/24
Canvas, 65 x 81.5 cm
Acquired 1926. Property of the
Kaiser Friedrich-Museums-Verein

Buytewech, called "de gheestige Willem" (witty Willem) by his contemporaries, was a master above all of graphic
techniques. Only eight paintings have
been identified as his; similar, elegantly
mobile figures appear in all of them. The
Berlin composition with six figures in
an interior is arranged symmetrically
like a stage set. The spontaneous situation of this "cheerful company" is captured with lively brushstrokes, in bright
colours based on blue, red and yellow.
Loose social scenes of this kind also had
a pedagogic intention. They revealed
the much-castigated, dissipated life of
the prosperous younger generation. Our
picture also contains the allegory of the
"Five Senses".   *IG*

Roelant Savery   (1576–1639)

124   Paradise, 1626
Oak, 80.5 x 137.6 cm
Acquired 1829

This picture was given to Princess Ama-
lie von Solms as a wedding present on
21 December, 1626. The composition is
appropriate to the late Mannerist view
of landscape. Another component of the
spatial depth is created by a diagonal of
light shining in from the top left, which
makes the countless birds stand out effectively in their lightness against the
highly conspicuous numbers of large and
small animals on the ground. They are all
crowded close together in a number of
positions, reproduced with conscientious
zoological accuracy, set in plant-life that
is equally faithfully recorded. A dodo can

be seen bottom right, a flightless bird brought to Europe by Dutch sailors in 1598. In the background is the first human couple in the Fall of Man.　　IG

Esaias van de Velde
(1590/91–1630)

125 Cheerful Gathering on a Garden Terrace, c. 1620
Canvas, 43 x 77 cm
Acquired 1918

Esaias van de Velde is one of the pioneers of naturalistic Dutch landscape painting. He also painted genre pictures, preferably banquets, often with a moralising undertone. There is a suggestion of mildly depraved behaviour in the flirting couple on the left of the table, and in the foppish officer on the right, who are all made conspicuous by colour and light. On the right, a view opens up to a garden which is thematically reminiscent of the medieval garden of love. The column was a traditional symbol of steadfastness, and the pitcher for washing on the far right stands for cleanliness.　　CB

Frans Hals　(1581/85–1666)

126 Singing Boy with Flute,
c. 1623/25
Canvas, 62 x 54.5 cm
Acquired 1874

This head-and-shoulders portrait shows a boy holding a flute in his right hand. His head is inclined slightly to the side, and he seems to be listening to the sound of his music—the raised left hand reinforces this intention. The spontaneous, flatly applied brushline is typical of Hals, who frequently painted cheerful children, often making music. The picture type, the handling of light and the boy's theatrical costume clearly show the influence of Caravaggio's followers in Utrecht.　　CB

Frans Hals   (1581/85–1666)

127   Catharina Hooft with her Nurse
c. 1619/20
Canvas, 86 x 65 cm
Acquired 1874

Frans Hals is one of the most influential
Dutch portrait painters before Rembrandt. He painted Catharina, who came
from a family of lawyers, in 1620; she
was about two years old at the time. Her
status is underlined by the lavish use
of lace on her brocade clothing, which
contrasts starkly with the nurse's mod-
est garb. The ambitious composition
is reminiscent of formal portraits, but
Hals always painted his subjects, most of
whom came from his social circle, in a
very life-like fashion.   *CB*

Frans Hals   (1581/85–1666)

128   Malle Babbe, c. 1633/35
Canvas, 75 x 64 cm
Acquired 1874

Malle Babbe ("malle" means mad) is
undoubtedly one of Hals's masterpieces.
The powerful handling of paint conveys
emotion, spontaneity and a natural quality in a virtuose fashion. The complex
movement underlines this effect. The owl
indicates a second level of meaning. It
was seen as a symbol of wisdom, but as
a night bird it also stood for the darker
sides of human behaviour, like stupid-
ity and drunkenness. The prominently
placed pewter tankard leaves no doubt
about which vice is meant here.   *CB*

Frans Hals   (1581/85–1666)

129   Portrait of Tyman Oosdorp,
1656
Canvas, 89 x 70 cm
Acquired 1877

Tyman Oosdorp was a member of
Haarlem city council from 1651. This
portrait dating from 1656 has all the
typical features of Hals's late work: the
subject is uncommunicative, in a distant

and self-absorbed pose. The composition suggests that the artist is concentrating on conveying a thoughtful expression. The strongly lit face is more strongly modelled than the robe.   *CB*

Dirck Hals   (1591–1656)

130   Interior with Merry Table-Gathering, c. 1625/30
Oak, 27.6 x 43.5 cm
Acquired 1915

Dirck Hals specialised in painting "merry gatherings". His paintings reveal his familiarity with the work of his brother, Frans Hals, as well as that of Willem Buytewech, from whom he occasionally copied figure motifs. The Berlin composition, colourful and meticulously drawn, acquires a moral undertone from the presence of the little winged altarpiece in the next room. Its motif of Christ's crucifixion reminds the boisterous company at the table that they should be leading decorous and pious lives.   *CB*

Pieter Claesz   (1597/98–1660)

131   Still Life with Rummer and Silver Vessel, c. 1635
Oak, 42 x 59 cm
Acquired 1945

Pieter Claesz is one of the principal painters of "monochrome banketjes", a type of still life that relies on plain motifs, austere pictorial structure and reduced colouring.

Claesz's mastery in subtly recording the physical character of objects is revealed in the way in which he presents the rummer, half full of wine, the silver drinking vessel that has been knocked over and the two pewter plates.

This colour-coordinated painting based on grey, green and silver tones and the pyramid structure of the image give the picture its quality of completeness.   *CB*

Thomas de Keyser (1596/97–1667)

132   Portrait of a Lady, 1632
Oak, 79.1 x 52.4 cm
Acquired 1982

Although there is no definite information about the identity of the subject, her
clothing and surroundings clearly suggest
her high social standing. De Keyser, one
of the most prominent portrait painters
in Amsterdam, combines great care in
executing painterly detail with psychological perception of the woman. The
influence of Frans Hals is evident here,
as is that of Antwerp court portraiture.
The companion piece, *Portrait of a Man*,
is now in the Louvre.   *CB*

Balthasar van der Ast
(1593/94–1657)

133   Still Life with Basket of Fruit
Oak, 14.4 x 20.1 cm
Acquired 1916

This artist was a member of the so-called
Bosschaert Dynasty in Middelburg
in Zeeland, where the northern and
southern Netherlandish views of art
met fruitfully in about 1600. This group
of still-life painters based their painting
technique on the work of Ambrosius
Bosschaert the Elder, and influenced
Dutch still-life painting in Utrecht, and
Delft particularly. Van der Ast worked
in Delft from 1632, where his palette
lightened noticeably. The Berlin picture
shows the clear, light colours of this
period against an almost whitish-grey
ground, from which the lavish arrangement of fruit in a woven basket stands
out almost in silhouette. On the darker
area of the table are figs, a plum, exotic
shells and an immaculate cherry twig.
The microcosm recorded with the eyes
of a researcher is completed by small
creatures. The diversity of nature and the
juxtaposition of freshness and perishabil-
ity signal general praise of creation and
also the idea of transience as a secular
moral message.   *IG*

Pieter Jansz Saenredam
(1597–1665)

134 View into the Ambulatory of
St. Bavo in Haarlem, 1635
Wood, 48.2 x 37.1 cm
Acquired 1874

Saenredam was one of the first Dutch
painters to specialise in views and interiors of churches. His pictures are based
on preliminary studies constructed precisely according to the rules of perspective, and provide an exact image of the
building concerned. Religious connotations play a subordinate role; the staffage
figures, representing the Presentation
of Christ in the Temple, were added by
another hand.

The painter's claim to be a learned
artist was more by virtue of his knowledge of "mathematical science". The
light, yellowish-white colouring, which
emphasises the sober clarity and formal
austerity of his pictures, is typical of
Saenredam's late work. There are two
preliminary studies for this work in
Haarlem and London.   *CB*

Nicolaes Eliasz Pickenoy
(1588–1650/56)

135 Cornelis de Graeff, Mayor of
Amsterdam and his Wife Catherina
Hooft, 1636
Canvas, 185.2 x 105 cm
Acquired 1874

Larger-than-life full-figure portraits
were always considered a prestigious
aristocratic indulgence in Dutch portrait
painting, accorded only to extraordinarily honourable and wealthy families
in the bourgeois milieu. Cornelis de
Graeff, with his many influential offices,
was felt to be worthy of this. The portraits were apparently commissioned on
the occasion of de Graeff's marriage to
the daughter of the distinguished lawyer
Pieter de Hooft, and designed entirely
according to the classical topos of the
marital portrait. They are looking the
viewer straight in the eye, with expressionless faces and restrained gestures.
Pickenoy was not a ground-breaking
master. Nevertheless, he had access to the
most important portrait commissions of
top society in Amsterdam.   *IG*

effects in order to stress the conspiratorial nature of this betrayal scene. He creates a chiaroscuro that emphasises the figures and the colour of the garments, but at the same time locks them into their surroundings, which are reduced to light-brown tonal values and economical indications of form. Rembrandt's psychological grasp of the theme shows particularly in the Philistine, who is approaching reluctantly, with an anxious expression on his face, and in the solider who is looking out from behind the curtain.   *CB*

Rembrandt   (1606–1669)

137   Self-Portrait with Velvet Beret
1634
Oak, 58.3 x 47.5 cm
Acquired 1830

Numerous paintings and drawings show that Rembrandt was more interested in himself as a subject, from the earliest times and well into old age, than any other artist of his period. This portrait with a velvet beret is a manifestation of his self-confidence: he had married Saskia Uylenburgh in 1634, and thus above his station. It also shows that he was familiar with the famous Rubens self-portrait (Windsor Castle). But unlike Rubens, Rembrandt does not present himself as an honourable gentleman, but as an established painter, who is basing his self-representation on art, rather than social status. The beret is also one of the painter's typical attributes, and the alert turn of the head towards the viewer and the thoughtful look out of the picture had been standard to the portraiture of artists since the Renaissance.   *CB*

Rembrandt   (1606–1669)

136   Samson and Delilah, 1628 (?)
Oak, 61.4 x 50 cm
Acquired 1906

Rembrandt focused his composition on the dramatic climax of the story: the invincible Samson is sleeping in the lap of Delilah, who is going to reveal the secret of his superhuman strength to the advancing Philistine. She is pointing to Samson's hair, which is about to fall victim to the scissors. The spatial sequence of the figures corresponds to the time sequence in the Bible story (Judges 16, 4–22). The handling of light is crucial to the elucidation of the pictorial events. Rembrandt avoided strong lighting

Pieter Lastman   (1583–1633)

138   Susanna and the Elders, 1614
Oak, 42 x 58 cm
Acquired 1914

The Book of Daniel tells of the respected Joachim, who had a house with a garden

in Babylon, where the Jews used to meet. Among them were two old judges who were deeply attracted by Joachim's wife Susanna, and decided to surprise her one day while she was bathing in the garden. Susanna rejected them, and she was slandered and condemned to death.

Lastman shows Susanna, seated on a sphinx-like fountain, at the moment of being taken by surprise. The two elders have just approached, and are visibly impressed by her physical beauty. Two peacocks are sitting in the tree on the right, clearly relating to the judges as a traditional symbol of arrogance.　*CB*

Rembrandt　(1606–1669)

139　Susanna and the Elders, 1647
Mahogany, 76.6 x 92.7 cm
Acquired 1883

Technical examination of the picture has provided evidence of three versions, showing that Rembrandt was concerned with vivid impact when devising his images. In terms of composition he is clearly indebted to his teacher Lastman. One of the elders has approached Susanna and seized her garment. Susanna's posture is ambiguous: she might be either turning backwards, startled by the advances, or attempting to escape forwards into the water. Rembrandt captured the dramatic climax at this moment of hesitation. Susanna catches the viewer's eye, thus making him a witness of her harassment by the two elders.　*CB*

Rembrandt (1606–1669)

140 The Mennonite Preacher Anslo and his Wife, 1641
Canvas, 173.4 x 207.6 cm
Acquired 1894

Cornelis Claesz Anslo was a rich Amsterdam ship-owner and cloth merchant, and also a respected Mennonite preacher. He moved into a new house with his family in 1641, and commissioned the double portrait with his wife Aeltje Schonten on this occasion.

The fact that the figures are seen slightly from above, and that the vanishing point is therefore relatively low, indicates that the picture was originally intended to be hung high. The fur trimming on the couple's clothes and the handkerchief are signs of prosperity and wealth.

However, a key concern was to present Anslo in his function as a preacher. His mouth is slightly open, he is pointing to the open book with his left hand, and turning to his wife, who is inclining her head a little, as a sign that she is paying attention. The essential elements of this scene, the book, faces and hands, are emphasised by the handling of light, while the remainder is plunged into monumental chiaroscuro.

This impressive representation of speaking and listening is vivid evidence of the Reformation's view that the word is superior to the image. A specific reference to the admonition specific to the Mennonites (based on Matthew 18, 15-20) is provided by the wick-trimmer that can be seen behind the candle. According to Picinello this symbolises the "correctio fraterna", the brotherly admonition "that frees the soul from the clinging slime of confusion as the wick-trimmer the candles from the dripping wax".

The fact that the subjects are presented in situations typical to their activity gives this double portrait its direct and lively effect. Rembrandt's approach to this genre went well beyond the presentational forms current at the time. *CB*

Rembrandt (1606–1669)

141 Moses with the
Ten Commandments, 1659
Canvas, 1168.5 x 136.5 cm
Acquired from the Royal Palaces

Moses is clearly about to smash the stone
tablets, which he has just received, in
rage and sorrow over the golden calf that
has been erected in his absence. The skin
of his face is shining, though in fact this
is not mentioned until the tablets had
been handed over for the second and
final time. The writing on the tablets
seems to translate the prophet's inner
torment into outward distress. It is uncertain whether the *Jacob Wrestling with
the Angel* in Berlin, slightly smaller because the canvas has been cut down, was
intended as a companion piece. It is clear
that the pictures were painted at almost
the same time and are similar in content;
moreover, the figures in both works have
a similarly overwhelming presence. This
monumental quality derives not least
from the placing of the figures at the
front edge of the picture, from the almost
abstract handling of the background,
the highly expressive brushwork and
neglect of detail, as well as the reduced
colour range, which is taken to an almost
monochrome extreme in the "Moses".
The greyish veils emphasise the figure's
isolation. The accurate Hebrew transcrip-
tion, shows Rembrandt's characteristic
attention to detail.   *MW*

Rembrandt (1606–1669)

142 Joseph and Potiphar's Wife,
1655
Canvas, 113.5 x 90 cm
Acquired 1883

The narrative moment is shifted from
the seduction to the false accusation. The
matron, who has hardly removed any of
her clothes, is pointing to Joseph across
the brightly lit marital bed. Her husband
is looking at her more in sorrow than
in anger, and Joseph is gazing helplessly
upwards. The figures occupy scarcely half
the height of the picture, which is reminiscent of earlier compositions, while the
angular movements, the sparse indication
of spatial relations and the eminently
painterly character, evoking the late
works of Titian with the paint applied
as if with a palette knife, all signal the
late style. We can sense why Sir Thomas
Lawrence chose this particular picture
for his collection. There is a somewhat
weaker variant in Washington, signed and
dated in the same way. Neutron auto-
radiography suggests that there was once
a portrait on this canvas; but before the
paint was completely dry layers of paint
were removed. The half-figure of an old
man roughly followed a preliminary
drawing in Dresden. This now hidden
portrait was also signed, and dated to the
same year. *MW*

Rembrandt (1606–1669)

143 Portrait of Hendrickje Stoffels
c. 1659
Canvas, 88.5 x 67 cm
Acquired 1879

A woman is leaning on the half-open
door, looking at the viewer with her
head slightly inclined. The informal pose
and dress—a housecoat, glowing deep
red in places and tied casually over the
low-cut white undergarment— suggest a
familiar relationship between painter and
model. For this reason the woman was
identified as his later companion Hendrickje Stoffels. The fact that Rembrandt
also had her sit for other paintings sup-
ports this interpretation.

The pictorial type reveals his familiarity with Palma Vecchio's portraits of
courtesans. This is confirmed by sci-
entific investigations showing that the
movement of the right arm originally
corresponded with the Venetian model,
but was then increasingly modified.
While the ring on Hendrickje's chain
gives her the status of a married woman,
the courtesan's pose reflects the extra-
marital relationship disapproved of by the
church. *CB*

Rembrandt, circle of
(1606–1669)

144 The Man with the Golden
Helmet, c. 1650/55
Canvas, 67.5 x 50.7 cm
Acquired 1897. Property of the
Kaiser Friedrich-Museums-Verein

Despite the popularity of *The Man with
the Golden Helmet*, which was attributed
to Rembrandt, there has been an increasing body of evidence casting doubt on its
authorship since the 1960s. The picture
was restored in the 1980s, and subjected
to a thorough technical examination,
which supported the reservations that
had been expressed in terms of style.

The helmet with its thickly applied
paint and sharply reflected light particularly show how Rembrandt's expressive
devices have been exaggerated. The dark,
almost graphic presentation of the face
is also not compatible with Rembrandt's
signature style.

The technical and stylistic differences
are revealed very clearly in a comparison with Rembrandt's painting *Man in
Armour* in Glasgow. In terms of content,
The Man with the Golden Helmet could be
interpreted as representing Mars, the god
of war, as a magnificent shining helmet
had long been seen as his attribute. This
theme was often taken up by painters in
Rembrandt's circle. The self-absorbed
expression on the subject's face has also
been linked with the motif of the sleeping Mars, symbolising silent weapons,
and thus peace.   *CB*

theme. The Berlin picture is an outstanding example of Dou's mature style: the
enamel-like smooth finish shows no
signs of brushwork.

His ability to capture the physical
qualities of objects is subtly revealed in
individual motifs. Thus the mother's velvet housecoat is painted with a different
technique than is the rough weave of the
curtain. Joachim von Sandrart reported
that Dou often worked with the aid of a
magnifying glass.   *CB*

Gerard Dou   (1613–1675)

145 The Young Mother, c. 1650
Wood, 49.2 x 37.4 cm
Acquired 1974. Property of the Kaiser
Friedrich-Museums-Verein

Gerard Dou was one of Rembrandt's
most important pupils and founded the
so-called Leiden school of painting. He
regularly addressed scenes of everyday
bourgeois life in small genre paintings,
including the popular mother-and-child

in the wall niche—handwashing utensils and secularised symbols of purity—fall within this pictorial concept. The painterly chiaroscuro with some colour accents, the sophisticated portrayal of the old woman, the contemplative effect emanating from the figure and the room are entirely within the tradition of Rembrandt, of whom Maes was one of the most talented pupils.   *CB*

Nicolaes Maes   (1634–1693)

146   Old Woman Peeling an Apple
c. 1655
Canvas, 55 x 50 cm
Acquired 1899

Nicolaes Maes started as a history painter, then switched to genre work as his main interest in the 1650s and then became one of the most respected portrait painters in Amsterdam. His genre pictures usually show interiors with scenes of everyday domestic life. Here an old woman is sitting by the window in a modestly furnished room and peeling an apple. This motif of a woman peeling an apple often occurs in Dutch painting, and was perceived as a symbol of virtuous living. The open book, the spinning wheel and above all the vessels

Gerard ter Borch   (1617–1681)

147   "Paternal Admonition"
c. 1654/55
Canvas, 71.4 x 62.1 cm
Acquired 1815

This is one of ter Borch's best-known works, and owes its familiarity and its misleading title to a 1765 reproduction engraving by Johann G. Wille. Goethe used the "Paternal Admonition" as the basis for an account of a soirée in *Elective Affinities*. But in fact this is not a family scene in a middle-class private house but a visit to a brothel.

The young officer's suggestive pose and gestures leave no doubt about this. The contrast between the depraved associations of the subject matter and the refined reticent presentation is a concession to bourgeois propriety. The reticence of the figures is typical of ter Borch, and so is the artful arrangement, which prevents them from entering into any communicative relationship with the viewer.

The actual focal point of the picture is the female figure, with her back to the viewer and dressed in a rich satin garment. Ter Borch exhibits technical virtuosity in rendering fabric, an ability which was highly praised by his contemporaries.   *CB*

Pieter de Hooch (1629 c. 1684)

148 The Mother, c. 1661/63
Canvas, 95.2 x 102.5 cm
Acquired 1876

De Hooch's early work consisted mainly of scenes in inns or events involving soldiers. After moving to Delft in 1654 he painted quiet garden courtyards and domestic interiors. This change of style derived from the artistic environment in Delft, where eminent artists like Jan Steen and Vermeer were working at the time.

De Hooch has something in common with Vermeer's work in particular. Both painters worked with similar subjects, and were interested in perspective, in painting light and rendering fabrics. In de Hooch's interiors the perspective almost always opens up via the sequence of rooms.

Starting with the room in the foreground, which seems to enclose the viewer, the eye moves outside either through an open door or a window, or into another room, before coming to rest outdoors. The sunlight helps to enhance the spatial illusion by illuminating people and objects with varying degrees of intensity, and by its reflection in the tiled floor.

De Hooch frequently shows women carrying out an everyday task: here a young mother is feeding her child. The gesture of opening or closing the bodice, the dog lingering curiously by its mistress, the little girl about to go outside through the open door—all of these details give the picture the quality of a snapshot. But they do not just depict the action; they also have a structural purpose and help to clarify the picture's three-dimensional organisation.   *CB*

Emanuel de Witte (1616/18–1692)

149 Interior of the Nieuwe Kerk in
Amsterdam, c. 1680
Canvas, 83 x 67 cm
Acquired 1874

Influenced by the architectural painters
of Delft, de Witte produced atmospheric
church interiors that try to include the
viewer in the picture by using unusual
perspectives and bold intersections. The
Berlin picture shows the interior of
the Nieuwe Kerk in Amsterdam from
the south transept, but it is not always
possible to assign de Witte's work to a
particular church. Frequently the views

are imaginary. His compositions rely on
the principle of "two–point perspective",
modelled on Hans Vredemann de Vries's
book on perspective, *Architectura*, which
was much consulted at the time. The
effect of the light streaming in through
the numerous windows is also captured
in a masterly fashion.   CB

Jan Vermeer van Delft
(1632–1675)

150 Young Woman with a Pearl
Necklace, c. 1662/65
Canvas, 55 x 45 cm
Acquired 1874

A young woman is standing by a table
and looking into a mirror to arrange
her pearl necklace. Light floods into
the room through the leaded window.
The yellow of the curtain and the fur-
trimmed jacket, and also the bare, white
wall—a masterpiece of pure painting in
the fine nuances of its colouring—create
an intense sense of colour that is addi-
tionally enhanced by the dark, blue-black
foreground.

Vermeer is one of the most famous
Dutch artists, despite the fact that his
oeuvre consists of only about thirty-five
paintings. He used perspective as an
important compositional and expressive
device.

Here the vanishing-point is just
above the table-top, and thus below the
subject's eye-level. This creates a kind of
worm's-eye view that helps to monu-
mentalise the figure and the objects.
Vermeer achieves the effect of depth by
allowing the edge of the picture to cut
through the chair, thus also increasing
the sense of intimacy. Close-up views
like this of people going about their
daily lives are a favourite subject for
Vermeer.

The bare wall becomes a field of tension that mediates between the woman
and the mirror and makes her look more
intense. This motif in Dutch painting
can be traced back as far as Hieronymus
Bosch. Mirrors were considered a traditional symbol of pride, and invoked

the pettiness and transience of worldly things. The pearls are a costly possession that can also be associated with vanity. *CB*

Jan Vermeer van Delft (1632–1675)

151 The Glass of Wine c. 1661/62
Canvas, 66.3 x 76.5 cm
Acquired 1901

An elegantly dressed young man is watching a woman finish a glass of wine. He has his hand on a jug, and seems to be waiting to refill the glass. Vermeer has taken the traditional motif of "wine, women and song", and, obviously influenced by a picture of ter Borch's, transformed it into a distinguished tête-à-tête.

In ter Borch's painting the cavalier had his arm around the woman's shoulder, but Vermeer does not give any explicit indication of the nature of this couple's relationship. It is uncertain whether consuming alcohol will lead to excess.

Vermeer simply provides hints. The chitarrone on the chair, an instrument that frequently occurs in his pictures, symbolises both harmony and frivolity. The window pane with the coat of arms also shows a woman holding a bridle, an attribute of Temperantia (moderation).

Vermeer handles the light coming in through the leaded window and its interplay with people and objects in a masterly fashion. In his later paintings in particular Vermeer used the "camera obscura", which opened up completely new opportunities for expression and design for artists, in order to capture the effect of light and colours more effectively. *CB*

Gabriel Metsu (1629–1667)

152 The Family of Gillis Valckenier,
Mayor of Amsterdam, c. 1657
Canvas, 72 x 29 cm
Acquired 1832

A patrician family has assembled in their
magnificent living-room. The fireplace
in ancient style, the gold leather wall-
covering, the lavishly detailed doorframe
and the large paintings are all signs of
prosperity.

The family has been identified as that
of Dr. Gillis Valckenier (1623–1680), the
mayor of Amsterdam. He, as the head of
the family, is majestically enthroned by
the table. His son is placed at his side,
with a parrot sitting on his outstretched
left arm. The lady of the house is surrounded by her daughters, and the nurse
on the right is holding the youngest
member of the family. The dog, a symbol
of faithfulness, is a frequent attribute on
pictures of families and married couples.

After Metsu moved to Amsterdam (in
about 1656), ter Borch became his most
important model, and he followed his
pictures in both choice of subject and
composition. His earlier, more dynami-
cally structured social scenes gave way
as in the Berlin picture to a more static
and less subtle arrangement of figures.
The painting clearly owes a great deal to
French taste, which was becoming more
influential in Holland, in its refined ap-
plication of paint and wealth of decorative detail. The borders between portrait
and genre painting have started to break
down. With this new approach, Metsu
is anticipating the French conversation
pieces that were so popular in the 18th
century.   CB

Jan Steen (1625/26–1679)

153 The Garden at the Inn, c. 1660
Canvas, 68 x 58 cm
Acquired 1830

In the 17th century it was the custom
to conclude an excursion with a stop at
the garden of an inn. In the foreground,
Steen shows a family having supper in
the shade of a pergola in great detail: the
mother is giving the child a drink from
a pewter tankard, the man on the left
(the father?) is skinning a herring, which
the dog is eyeing hungrily. Behind the
table is a fishmonger with a basket full
of shrimp and dried fish hanging over
his shoulder. The side lighting enhances
the impression of a peaceful evening

mood that emanates from the picture.
Inn scenes are a regular feature of Steen's
work, which extends from landscapes
via portraits to biblical history paintings.
The usual burlesque explicitness of the
way in which he depicts people gives
way here to showing the visitors enjoy-
ing their food and drink in each other's
company. For this reason we cannot be
sure whether Steen had any moral and
didactic intention in showing the mother
giving her child beer to drink.   *CB*

Jan Steen   (1625/26–1675)

154   Quarrel over a Game of Cards
c.1604/65
Canvas, 90 x 19 cm
Acquired 1874

A group of card-players have started
quarrelling outside a country inn.
Playing-cards, a backgammon set and a
pewter tankard have fallen to the floor.
The figures are designed carefully, with
a degree of painterly refinement, but
their surroundings are approached in a
somewhat cursory fashion. This kind of
picture goes back to Jan Steen's teacher
Adriaen van Ostade and beyond him to
Adriaen Brouwer and Pieter Bruegel the
Elder. The composition is held together
primarily by the element of movement,
exaggerated gestures and facial expressions that are typical of Steen's late style,
rather than by three-dimensional structure. Another typical feature is that his
later work tends to be larger and more
monumental, which can be traced back
to Jacob Jordaens's influence. Many of
Steen's genre paintings are inclined to
rather heavy moralising, the intent being
to illustrate poor conduct. The quarrelling men are an embodiment of Ire, one

of the seven deadly sins, or Discordia as
a result of addiction to gambling and
alcohol. This was a common and traditional subject-matter for painting, and
its symbols were familiar to all. Certainly
the moral lesson is presented to the
viewer with stage-like theatricality. The
furious man with his sword drawn is
reminiscent of Capitano, the anti-hero
of the commedia dell'arte. In order to
emphasise the narrative content of the
scene, Steen often drew on contemporary theatre for his pictorial vocabulary
and composition.   *CB*

Hercules Seghers   1589/90–1638)

155   Lowland Landscape with a
Town on a River, c. 1625/30
Oak, 27.2 x 36.2 cm
Acquired 1874

Seghers, in his small number of paintings,
was one of the first to show the broad
sweep of the Dutch lowlands consistently
in panoramic views. The low horizon
and the big sky—a strip was subsequently added to the top of the picture, to
enhance its effect—make the landscape
typically Dutch in character; the mirror-

image view of the town of Rhenen further adds to its reality. Seghers was also one of the most innovative landscape etchers of his day, and experimented with the possibilities of colour prints. *CB*

terial. Nevertheless, though his pictures seem extremely lifelike, they make no claims to topographical precision.

The space is opened up in terms of perspective by the river, which runs diagonally into the depths of the picture, a typical structural principle for van Goyen. The composition is held together by the atmospheric colouring, based on shades of yellow, brown and green.

A great deal of attention is also paid to the presentation of the sky. *CB*

Jan van Goyen (1596–1656)

156 View of Nijmegen, 1649
Oak, 67.7 x 97.8 cm
Acquired 1874

The town of Nijmegen with the landmark square tower of the Valkenhof rises above the right bank of the Waal. Town views are a major theme in van Goyen's work; he travelled a great deal, and was able to rely on his sketch-books for ma-

Salomon van Ruysdael
(c. 1600/03–1670)

157 Dutch Landscape with
Plunderers, 1656
Canvas, 106 x 148 cm
Acquired 1870

Approaching in the foreground is a
group of riders, who are leading stolen
cattle and peasants in chains. At the bottom of the picture shots are being fired
at people running away. The people have
a narrative function; but they are part of
a faceless crowd, and one of their addi-
tional functions is to give the painting a
sense of depth. The painting is structured
by strong contrasts between horizontal
and vertical elements: the line of the

horizon is kept low, and thus suggests
extreme distance, while the trees towering high into the sky give an impression
of direct proximity. The cloudy sky is
very important to van Ruysdael, as indeed it was to van Goyen. The sky could
not have been painted like this without
attention to nature. Works like these,
which are strikingly "compositional" in
style, mark the start of the classical period of Dutch landscape painting, which
replaced the tonal phase with its often
simple diagonal compositions from the
mid-17th century.   *CB*

Isack van Ostade   (1621–1649)

158 Winter Landscape with Sledges
and Boats Frozen in the Ice, c. 1645
Oak, 21 x 24.5 cm
Acquired 1913

Isack was influenced by his brother
Adriaen, who was also his teacher, and
preferred to paint scenes from everyday
peasant life. In his early scenes the figures were the key feature, but in his later
work the landscape becomes increasingly significant. Winter landscapes and
gatherings at inns are among the young
painter's principal subjects; he died at

an early age. The Berlin picture's theme is the winter landscape itself, which is atmospherically conveyed by the cloudy sky with its finely nuanced colouring, the weather, which becomes more severe towards the horizon, the town, which can be seen only in shadowy outline, and the ice-skaters in the distance. Isack van Ostade was primarily a genre painter, but his poetic pictures like this, which do not just reproduce local natural phenomena realistically, made an important contribution to Dutch landscape painting.   *CB*

Philips Wouwerman   (1619–1668)

159 Winter Landscape with Wooden Bridge, c. 1660
Oak, 28.5 x 36.5 cm
Acquired 1908

Philips Wouwerman, who according to Cornelis de Bie was taught by Frans Hals, was a much-admired painter of equestrian scenes, history pictures and landscapes in his day. His relatively small-scale works sold for high prices and made Wouwerman unusually rich for a painter. His equestrian scenes in particular were still popular with aristocratic collectors in the 18th century.

Wouwerman's landscapes contain numerous variations on the wooden bridge, a motif drawn from Flemish painting. Here the bridge fits into the composition parallel with the picture and restricts the view into the distance. It also covers up the huge cumulus snow-cloud that seems to be moving further and further into the foreground, linking with the blue-grey sky to convey a gloomy winter's day on which a few people have risked coming out into the open air to play or to do essential work.   *CB*

Jacob van Ruisdael
(c. 1628/29–1682)

160 Dam Square in Amsterdam
c.1675–80
Canvas, 52 x 65 cm
Acquired 1874

Dutch landscape painting reached its apogee in Jacob van Ruisdael, who combined natural composition with expressive statement in a masterly fashion in his pictures. Alongside this subject, he developed a growing interest in the city of Amsterdam as a pictorial motif at the end of his working life. Ruisdael was entirely familiar with the view shown here, as he lived on the south side of Dam Square from 1670. The square was dominated by the old Amsterdam municipal weighbridge; several bales of goods have already been placed under its canopy to be weighed. On the right the view opens up to the Damrak with its sailing-boats and the tower of the Oude Kerk. The square is enlivened by an unusually large number of figures, but van Ruisdael did not paint these himself—he was not an established figure specialist. They are pre-

sumably the work of Gerard van Battem, a painter from Rotterdam. The pale light from the left, the long shadows darkening the front of the square and the silvery-cool colour tones give the impression of a day that is only just beginning. *CB*

Jacob van Ruisdael
(c. 1628/29–1682)

161 Landscape with a View of Haarlem, c. 1670/75
Canvas, 52 x 65 cm
Acquired 1874

Ruisdael painted his birthplace, Haarlem, about fifteen times; these paintings are sometimes called "haarlempjes". They are all panoramic landscapes, in which the city and its churches, including the towering St. Bavo Kerk, are visible in the distance. In the foreground of this picture are the Haarlem bleaching-fields. Linen imported from other countries (including England) was bleached here and then put on the market. Haarlem grew to be the centre of this branch of the industry, to which it owed its growing prosperity.

Presenting this particular trade helps to identify the view of the town and at the same time symbolises the source of its wealth. The cloudy sky arches over the town, occupying about two thirds of the surface of the picture. Gathering cumulus clouds break up the light, so that the town below them is lit only in part. This interplay of light and shade reinforces the impression of breadth, which is also enhanced by the high placing of the horizon. The clarity and simplicity of the structure and the portrayal of the climatic mood put Ruisdael's "haarlempjes" among the major achievements of Dutch landscape painting.   *CB*

The composition is enlivened by large cumulus clouds with the sun shining on them, creating a varied play of light on the surface of the water. Even without a specific theme, apparently simple marine pieces of this kind could express the viewer's sense of national identity and also serve as a positive metaphor for man's harmony with God-determined nature.   *CB*

Ludolf Backhuysen   (1631–1708)

162   Choppy Sea with Ships, 1664
Canvas, 57.5 x 98.4 cm
Acquired from the Royal Palaces, 1829

Maritime painting was important to 17th-century Dutch art, as it was due to its shipping that the Dutch republic became a great naval and commercial power. Ludolf Backhuysen was one of the leading exponents of this genre. Various ships, representing the various branches of Dutch seamanship, are sailing on the slightly choppy sea: inland yachts, fishing boats, cargo vessels and warships. Many of them are flying the Dutch flag.

Meindert Hobbema (1638–1709)

163 Village Street Lined with Trees
c. 1663
Canvas, 97 x 128.5 cm
Acquired 1926

As in many of Hobbema's paintings, a sandy path leading into the picture is the key element of the composition. The luxuriantly leafy deciduous trees are painted in a manner reminiscent of Jacob van Ruisdael, who was Hobbema's teacher. But unlike Ruisdael, Hobbema does not emphasise the mystery and loneliness of the wood, but presents nature idyllically and peacefully. The sunny atmosphere and the light clouds convey a cheerful atmosphere of the kind a city-dweller might experience while walking in the woods. However, his work was not greatly appreciated until it was taken up by 18th-century and 19th-century landscape painters. *CB*

Willem Kalf (1619–1693)

164 Still Life with Chinese Porcelain Box, 1662
Canvas, 64 x 53 cm
Acquired 1899

Kalf's sumptuous still lifes use requisites appropriate to prosperity, and show a knowledge of foreign cultures. Oranges and lemons in a bowl perched on the edge of a table and Chinese porcelain are typical Kalf motifs.

The costly nature of the objects is duly reflected in the richness of the painting; the subtlety of the sparkling light and the warm colours were intensified by Kalf in a way that has never been surpassed. *CB*

Giotto di Bondone   (c. 1267–1337)

165   The Entombment of Mary c. 1310
Poplar, 75 x 179 cm
Acquired 1914. Property of the
Kaiser Friedrich-Museums-Verein

This piece was Bode's last acquisition
in the field of Trecento painting, which
added to the already rich holdings from
the Solly collection.

It is one of four panels described by
Lorenzo Ghiberti in 1445/55 as being
in the possession of the Frati Umiliati,
who owned the church and monastery
of Ognisanti. Giorgio Vasari praised the
piece in 1568, and quoted Michelangelo,
who said "that the particular quality of
this history could not have been represented more naturally or more faithfully".

The horizontal format with gable top
is similar to late 13th-century Tuscan
dossals, replaced after 1300 by polyptychs
and vertical-format altar-pieces. Research
has revealed that this panel was primarily
painted by Giotto himself. By comparison to his *Maestà* in the Uffizi Gallery
this work is dated c. 1310.   *HN*

Maso di Banco
(2nd quarter of the 14th century)

166   Mary with the Child,
c. 1335/36
Poplar, 81.5 x 49.2 cm
Acquired 1821

This centre panel from a five-part altarpiece was possibly painted for the

Franciscan Order; scholars have considered the church of S. Croce in Florence,
where there are still some of the master's
works today. He came from the school
of Giotto, but combined compact forms
and strict outlines with a subtle linearity
of detail, refined tonality and decorative
harmony of colour areas, ornaments
and a chased gold ground. Scholars see
the representation of three-quarter figures as the transition to altars with full
figures.   *HN*

Taddeo Gaddi
(late 13th century? −1366)

167 The Outpouring of the Holy
Spirit; St. Francis Wakens a Child
c. 1335/45
Walnut, 46 x 38.2 cm; 48.2 x 43 cm
Acquired 1828/29

These panels were part of juxtaposed
scenes from the Life of Christ and his
"follower" St. Francis, which were part
of the furniture decoration in the sacristy
of S. Croce in Florence. Its creator was in
the tradition of Giotto. But in comparison it is clear that Taddeo's figures tend
not so much to "plumb" the space, as to
make dramatic events tangible through
dynamic grouping and accentuated gestures. Synchronised presentations portray
different movements within a particular
period of time. *HN*

Lippo Memmi
(shortly after 1290–1356)

168 Mary with the Child, c. 1330
Poplar, 86.5 x 55 cm
Acquired 1843

Orthodox traditions still largely govern
the pose and clothing of Mary and the
child here. In the course of the 13th and
14th centuries new values developed in
the way the two were juxtaposed: the

mother turns lovingly to the child, rather than facing the viewer to command reverence, there is an expression of melancholy and the boy's pose is more childlike. He is looking out of the picture in such a way that scholars feel justified in assuming that the panel formed the centre of an altarpiece created on the model of Simone Martini with studio participation by Lippo.   *HN*

Bernardo Daddi
(late 13th century –1348)

169   Altar Panel in the Form of a Triptych, c. 1338/40
Poplar, 58 x 57.2 cm
Acquired 1821

In the second half of the 14th century Bernardo's studio produced polyptychs and small portable altars and votive images, based on familiar iconographic motifs. But as time passed various in-

fluences and changed artistic attitudes made themselves felt. Christ's birth and death are significantly juxtaposed. The role of the virgin Mother of God as the Bride of Christ and Queen of Heaven is confirmed by her coronation. This motif developed, emanating from the Orthodox church, in Siena in the 14th century. This little altar uses the pictorial surfaces in a superior way to comparable versions: they are no longer subdivided; landscapes and architectural elements identify the location like set-pieces, and a new interest in spatial quality can also be discerned.   *HN*

Pietro Lorenzetti
(active 1306? –1348)

170 St. Humilitas Cures a Sick Nun;
The Ice Miracle of St. Humilitas
c. 1330/35
Poplar, 46.2 x 55.4 cm; poplar, transferred
to canvas, 43.5 x 33.7 cm
Acquired 1821; 1888

Rosana Negosanti (c. 1226–1310) of
Faenza took the name "Humilitas" after
entering the Convent of St. Perpetua.
Later she was abbess of the Vallumbro-
sian convent of St. John the Apostle near
Florence. The Sienese Pietro Lorenzetti
created the altar in the church. The centre panel shows the saint towering up
like a statue, surrounded by scenes from
her life. The two Berlin pieces, presumably from the lower row, narrate the
healing of a sister when medical knowledge had failed, and how suffering was
eased by ice, which was still to be found
in the well in August. People carrying
out miraculous deeds are so important
that they are disproportionately larger
in the stage-like, boxy rooms. Certain
situations are furnished like set-pieces,
and the perspective is well observed,
but not yet calculated. Areas of light and
shade underline an effective structure,
but the expressive gestures of the figures
are always shown against a calm background.   *HN*

Simone Martini (c. 1284–1344)

171 The Entombment of Christ
Poplar, 23.7 x 16.7 cm
Acquired 1901

Simone Martini is the purest embodiment of 14th-century Sienese art. He
combines elegance of line, colours that
glow like jewels and technical brilliance
with sharp observation of nature and
psychological sensitivity. At the papal
court in Avignon he created a small
travelling altar with Passion scenes, to
which the Berlin panel belonged. Parts
of the signature are or used to be found
on the slats of the frame. The patron was

probably Cardinal Napoleone Orsini. The surface of the picture has also been altered; there is an original gold ground under the reddish evening sky.   HN

Gentile da Fabriano
(c. 1370?–1427)

172   Mary Enthroned with the Child, Saints and a Donor
Poplar, 131 x 113 cm
Acquired 1837

Gentile da Fabriano was considered to be one of the leading masters of International Gothic in Italy. The Berlin picture is probably the earliest of Gentile's surviving works, painted at the beginning of his career for the church of San Niccolò in Fabriano, without his having had to seek out other artistic centres. The composition takes the form of a "Sacra Conversazione". Mary is sitting on a bench throne. The Christ Child is standing on her lap and blessing the donor, who is kneeling to the left (on a smaller scale), and whom the church's titular saint is commending to the Madonna. The picture was removed from the church c. 1630.   HN

Lorenzo Monaco
(c. 1365–before 1426)

173   The Birth of Christ
c. 1395/1400
Poplar, 26.3 x 60.7 cm
Acquired 1821

Lorenzo Monaco worked in the painters' studio of the Florentine monastery of S. Maria degli Angeli. The Berlin scene was recognised as the centre panel of the predella of a work from S. Maria del Carmine. In terms of content this relates to the central depiction of the Madonna in the main section. The child is not in the manger, but is being presented on his mother's lap, as in the centre panel: there he is in splendour as the Son of God, here part of the scene, as a human child. Ox and ass can be related to a prophecy by Isaiah: "The ox knows its owner, and the ass its master's crib; but Israel does not know, my people does not understand." The sleeping Joseph and the ruined building in the background are seen as representing the old covenant between God and man to which the prophet is referring.   HN

Masaccio (1401–1428?)

174 The Crucifixion of the Apostle
Peter; The Beheading of John the
Baptist; The Adoration of the Kings
(Altar Predella), 1426
Poplar, each panel 21 x 61 cm
Acquired 1880

Masaccio was the first of the early Renaissance painters. He consistently used
central perspective in painting, and
moved beyond medieval representation
of three dimensions. His figures, powerful in their three-dimensional physical
presence, seem monumental and act
on a uniform spatial stage, with effects
enhanced by logical handling of light.
The altar for S. Maria del Carmine in
Pisa, painted in 1426 for notary Ser
Giuliano di Colino degli Scarsi da San
Giusto, is one of the principal works
of his short career. Only the *Madonna
Enthroned with Angels* has survived from
the principal section (London, National
Gallery). The Berlin Gemäldegalerie has
four figures of saints from the side pilasters and the predella, which has survived
intact. The left-hand panel shows the
martyrdoms of St. Peter and St. John
the Baptist. Masaccio's masterpiece is
undoubtedly the long central panel with

the Three Kings. Behind the youngest
of them, in profile only two men in
bourgeois clothing with portrait-like
features are calmly watching the
event—clearly the man who commissioned the work, with a member of his
family.   *HN*

Paolo Schiavo (1397–1478)

175 The Annunciation; St. Jerome;
St. Laurence
(Parts of a triptych) c. 1425/30
Poplar, centre panel 105 x 71 cm,
left panel 98.5 x 39.4 cm,
right panel 98.3 x 38.3 cm
Acquired 1821

The birth of Christ is proclaimed to
Mary by the Archangel Gabriel, and the
Almighty himself is sending the dove
of the Holy Spirit down to earth. Six-
winged seraphim form the halo. Mary is
identified as a pure virgin by the lilies in
the angel's band. St. Jerome, on the left-
hand panel, appears in his traditional garb
as a cardinal, in his quality as an ecclesias-
tical teacher. A lion has been his attribute
since the penitential period.

    St. Laurence, on the right, is always
depicted in a dalmatic; the instrument of

his torture, a gridiron, can be seen behind him. Paolo Schiavo's style bears the
marks of International Gothic, but here
is evidence of a new understanding of
pictorial organisation. *HN*

part in any other work by Piero as in the
Berlin picture. *HN*

Piero della Francesca
(c. 1420/22–1492)

176 The Penitent St. Jerome, 1450
Chestnut, 51.5 x 38 cm
Acquired 1922

After the First World War, Wilhelm von
Bode was able to acquire only two more
important work of early Italian Renaissance painting, one of which was this
signed and dated landscape with St.
Jerome by Piero della Francesca. Piero
painted the picture in Ferrara, where
he worked from 1449, perhaps from
1446/47, at the court of Lionello d'Este.
The little votive image did not seem to
be authentic for the most part in the
condition shown by von Bode; another
view held that it was incomplete. But
when it was restored from 1968 to 1972
Piero's original painting was revealed.
The figure had been most damaged by
earlier cleaning. The meticulous reproduction of detail and brilliance of colour
are reminiscent of Netherlandish work.
Landscape does not play as dominant a

Fra Angelico   (c. 1395?–1455)

177   The Last Judgement
Poplar, centre panel 102.8 x 65.2 cm,
left-hand wing 103 x 28.2 cm,
right-hand wing 102.7 x 28 cm
Acquired 1884

The Last Judgement is described in
the Revelation of St. John the Divine,
among other places. Our version may
originally have been a uniform panel.
This conclusion could be drawn from
the composition: it shows a continuous
pictorial space with fluent transitions.
Nevertheless the sections, appropriate to
the content and mood of these themes,
are treated differently in terms of colour
and composition. Christ is enthroned on
the seat of mercy as judge of the world.
With the sign of the cross, which an
angel is presenting as a reference to his
sacrificial death, he is promising forgiveness or condemnation to the risen. Mary
and John traditionally sit close to him, to
ask for grace for mankind. Representatives of the "old covenant", apostles and
saints are fellow judges in the court.
Didactic inscriptions appeal to the faith-

ful for contrition. All that is found on
the Paradise side is Christ's monogram
embroidered on an angel's robe. On the
Hell side pride is referred to in Latin as
the cardinal sin, and groups of people
are identified who have succumbed to
mortal sin. The drama of the Last Days
is characterised by narrative elements
and depicted emotions. Members of
various social groups are suggested in
the contemporary clothing of the risen.
Members of the Franciscan and Dominican Orders dominate: the altar was
presumably commissioned by clergy in
Rome.   *HN*

Domenico Veneziano
(c. 1405/10–1461)

178   The Adoration of the Kings
c. 1439/41
Poplar, diameter 84 cm
Acquired 1880

This tondo was probably owned by the
Medici. One stylistic feature is the influence of International Gothic, passed
on to Domenico from Pisanello. The

extravagant garments, painted with great virtuosity, were probably influenced by Pisanello—as were the numerous animal motifs—but they also follow the fashions of the day. Elements referring to late medieval chivalry, for example the mottoes, have been related to International Gothic; some link with the Medicis' patronage of the Compagnia de' Magi is also conceivable. Thus the Three Kings became "heraldic representatives" of the family. The portraits in their retinue are a matter of controversy. Piero, Cosimo and the young Giovanni de' Medici are among those considered. The way in which the scene is set in a landscape, projected deep into the pictorial space, is considered to be one of the tondo's major achievements.   *HN*

of the Holy Spirit. Thus the Trinity is depicted here, with the child defined as God the Son. His nakedness is frequently interpreted as a symbolic reference to the sacrifice of his death.   *HN*

Sassetta (c. 1400?–1450)

179   Mary with the Child,
c. 1432/36
Poplar, 50.8 x 29 cm
Presumably acquired 1821

It is probable that this centre panel from a triptych, whose other sections are in American collections, came to Berlin with the Solly Collection. This work demonstrates the style of the Sienese artist Sassetta particularly clearly: traditional two-dimensional composition remained important for him, fitting figures precisely into a format, the elegance of the outlines, the harmonious relationship of painted surfaces and the chased gold ground. Artistic resources of this calibre lend brilliance to the image of the Madonna. The type goes back to precisely determined Eastern models but in the course of development the original austerity gave way to human closeness, and this period's ideas of beauty were also transferred to images of the Madonna. The oriental seated motif was interpreted in the West as a sign of humility. Nevertheless Mary has the attributes of the Queen of Heaven: hovering angels hold her crown, and above them we can see God the Father, supported by cherubim and giving his blessing, and the dove

Master of the Osservanza
(2nd quarter of the 15th century)

180   The Mass of St. Anthony Abbas
c. 1435
Poplar, 46.8 x 33.4 cm
Acquired 1910

St. Anthony of Egypt was born in 251 in
Heraklea, Egypt, and died in 356. A sermon led to his renunciation of worldly
life. The Berlin panel is one of eight
surviving scenes from the saint's legend.
It is considered to be of particularly high
quality because the interior perspective
is so well observed—it is reminiscent of
Siena cathedral—, the architecture and
figures relate so harmoniously, the formal
language is lucid and the colours are
balanced, light and festive. It is noticeably
close to the style of Sassetta.   *HN*

Giovanni di Paolo
(worked 1420–1482)

181   The Crucifixion of Christ
c. 1440/45
Poplar, 40.1 x 56 cm
Acquired 1904. Property of the
Kaiser Friedrich-Museums-Verein

This small horizontal image was probably the centre panel of an altar predella:
here scenes from the New Testament
and from legends complemented and
commented upon the scenes in the main
section. We recognise the skull of Adam,
the blind soldier Longinus, the converted
captain. In late Gothic pictorial narratives
of this kind, fine observation of reality,
pleasure taken in detail and heightened
emotions "recall" the story of salvation.
                                           HN

Antonio del Pollaiuolo
(1431?–1498)

182   Profile Portrait of a Young
Woman, c. 1465
Poplar, 52.5 x 36.5 cm
Acquired 1897/98

Attribution to Pollaiuolo is largely accepted by recent scholarship. A minority think of Piero della Francesca, and the most recent monograph assigns it to anonymity, along with some related portraits. The attribution is based on the observation of stylistic features that are also achievements in terms of comparable pieces. This is one of the finest portraits of the early Florentine Renaissance in the purity of its line and subtle execution, in the nobility of the pose and the self-confident dignity of the woman's expression.   *HN*

Antonio del Pollaiuolo
(1431?–1498)

183   David as Victor, c. 1472
Poplar, 48.2 x 35 cm
Acquired 1890

The shepherd David, who defeated the giant Goliath, was a symbolic figure of Florence as an independent city state. Antonio Pollaiuolo, who worked as a painter, but also as a sculptor in bronze and marble, placed the confidently posing youth diagonally in a niche, like a statuette. His shadow falls on the neutral background of a wall that is scarcely articulated, enhancing the fluid lines and reticent colours. The period was interested in the ideal representation of human beings and the aim was to achieve a harmonious pictorial effect. This is also the case here: the fight is over, and David is given the sling and the enemy's head as his attributes.   *HN*

front of the interior, whose perspective structure is not as strict as it appears. The spatial effect is further enhanced by the minimal quantity of furniture. This is balanced by the brilliant treatment of the marble inlay of floors and walls (which was intended to be even more lavish at first), or the costly decoration of the bedchamber, which seems to be continued in the gold woven into Mary's garments, thus taking away even more of her physical presence. There is a view of Florence and the Tuscan hills, but the very opulence of the interior and the inconsistencies of perspective suggest that this was intended to be ideal rather than real architecture.   *MW*

Piero del Pollaiuolo
(1443?–1496?)

184   The Annunciation, c. 1470
Poplar, without frame 150.5 x 174.5 cm
Acquired 1821

There is scarcely another Quattrocento altar-piece in which the actual subject of the picture is so outshone by the contents in the background. The figures seem to "float" in the foreground in

Andrea del Castagno (c. 1421–1457)

185 The Assumption 1449/50
Poplar, 131 x 150.7 cm
Probably acquired 1821

This altar panel, painted for the little
Florentine church of S. Miniato fra le
Torre, is one of a group of works showing Mary's ascent into heaven—here
flanked by the patron saint, Minias, and
St. Julian—as a mature woman with her
head covered.

Brilliant drawing and complicated
movement are set against indistinct
spatial relations and an antiquated gold
ground. Vasari was one of the first to
identify "power in the movement of the
figures" as one of Castagno's qualities.
He left only a small body of work, but
was in many ways ahead of his times.

The idiosyncratic under-drawing
corresponds closely with the sinopia
for the somewhat earlier frescoes in
S. Apollonia.   *MW*

Fra Filippo Lippi (1406?–1469)

186 The Adoration in the Forest, c. 1459
Poplar, without frame 126.7 x 115.3 cm
Acquired 1821

This Adoration comes from the most
distinguished place imaginable: the
private chapel in the Palazzo Medici-
Riccardi, to which Benozzo Gozzoli's
famous fresco of the *Medici Family as
the Magi* (still in situ) led. Lippi created
this Adoration in about 1459. Variations
(Florence, Uffizi) were painted after
1453 and, again for the Medici, around
1463. This completely unusual scenario
in the depths of a dense forest and the
lavish details conceal at first how poorly
the perspective has been handled and
the antiquated treatment of the cracks
in the rocks. The unusual iconography
has scarcely anything in common with
traditionally narrated pictures of Christ's
birth. The boy John, looking thoughtfully out of the picture, and Bernard of
Clairvaux at prayer, prototypes of the
repentance-preacher and the hermit, emphasise the meditative atmosphere.   *MW*

Andrea del Verrocchio
(c. 1435–1488)

87   Mary with the Child, c. 1470
Poplar, 73.8 x 54.7 cm
Acquired 1873

Only two paintings have been definitely
attributed to Verrocchio. A group of
pictures of the Madonna is related to his
marble and terracotta reliefs. Only in the
case of the "Berlin Madonna" has a broad
consensus been established about attribution to Verrocchio himself. Scholars see
the influence of Antonio del Pollaiuolo
in features such as the marked spatial
quality, the rhythmic flow of line and the
powerful modelling. They also refer to
the dependence of Leonardo's "Munich
Madonna", c. 1476, on the one painted
by his teacher Verrocchio about six years
earlier.   *HN*

Sandro Botticelli (1445–1510)

188 Madonna with Saints,
1484/85
Poplar, 185 x 180 cm
Acquired 1829

This altar panel, one of Botticelli's most
carefully painted and best-preserved
paintings, was commissioned by the
Florentine merchant Giovanni d'Agnolo
de'Bardi for his burial chapel in S. Spirito. The original frame by Giuliano da
Sangallo was probably lost when the
picture, which stayed in the Bardi family
until 1825, was replaced by a more modern painting only a hundred years after
its installation. A copy of a similar period
frame in S. Spirito was created for this
work in 1978.

The subject matter, the enthroned
Madonna with saints standing at her side,
originates with Fra Angelico, and it was
the theme of several other altar paintings

(done at the same time or slightly earlier)
in S. Spirito. Here the saints are the two
St. Johns, with John the Baptist in the
place of honour as patron saint. Botticelli moves away from the other works
mentioned by reducing the architectural
constructs and making the baldacchino
behind Mary entirely of palm fronds.
Foliage niches allude to the earlier, tri-
partite retable type.

The composition is dominated by
the over-lavish plant decoration, even
though the countless texts (mainly from
Jesus Sirach), make it clear that it has a
very specific iconographical purpose.
This tension between precise observation of nature and an elaborate concept
is well served by elements that play down
the distance from the viewer: the eyes of
John the Baptist and the Christ Child,
the placing of the saints on the step leading into the image or the small crucifix
on the altar, which we imagine to be
beneath the painting. *MW*

Sandro Botticelli   (1445–1510)

189   Mary with the Child and Singing Angels, c. 1477
Poplar, diameter 135 cm
Acquired 1954

It is possible that this circular picture used to belong to the Brothers of S. Francesco in Florence. Mary is identified as the Queen of Heaven by a crown, but at the same time she is the mother of the boy Christ, who is marked out for sacrifice. He is reaching for her breast. Theologians saw Mary as the giver of nourishment, as the mother of all mankind, and of salvation. Singing angels are praising her, with lilies in their hands as symbols of purity. Just as the ideal of earthly female beauty was always sought in the face and form of Mary, in the same way the angels can be seen as embodying youthful harmony. Botticelli mastered this demanding format with a calculated pictorial order that takes up the circular border: the Madonna is enthroned at the centre of a multiple encircling movement.   HN

Francesco di Giorgio Martini, attributed to (1439–1501)

190   Architectural Veduta
c. 1490/1500
Poplar, 131 x 233 cm
Acquired 1896. Property of the Kaiser Friedrich-Museums-Verein

Comparably exceptional depictions of space are to be found only in two other collections: in Baltimore and Urbino. The unique quality of these three pieces within early Renaissance painting is constantly emphasised. They are seen as illustrations of constructions with a central perspective, of concrete town planning or also ideal variants on urban spatial organisation formulated in a spirit of Humanism. In the case of the Berlin panel reference is also made to a concurrent description of piers and docks in Francesco di Giorgio Martini's *Trattato di Architettura*. This piece was probably created in the cultural atmosphere of Urbino, where in the mature Quattrocento mathematics, painting, architecture and interior design were closely linked under Federico da Montefeltre. There are parallels with perspectives of this kind in intarsia work.   HN

Piero di Cosimo (1461/62–1521?)

191 Venus, Mars and Cupid
Poplar, 72 x 182 cm
Acquired 1828

Vasari himself chose to keep this picture
"in Piero's memory", because, in his own
words, "he always took pleasure in his
strange ideas". This picture may well have
been a marriage piece, as may well be the
case with Botticelli's almost equally great
treatment of the material (now in London, National Gallery). Cosimo moved
away from this obvious model by placing the figures more naturally in their
surroundings. This allows for a greater
degree of love symbolism in the way in
which Cupid, the rabbit or the billing
and cooing doves are built into the composition. Groups of amoretti are disappearing into the distance, carrying away
the weapons of the god of war, who
has succumbed to the goddess of love's
magic spell. Venus is largely naked, but
is not looking at her beloved with any
degree of expectancy. Looking beyond
the sexual connotations, the ancients, and
the neo-Platonists in particular, valued
the union of Venus and Mars philosoph-
ically as a symbol of nature's fertility and
a peacemaking combination of opposites,
which further justifies Piero's broad
depiction of nature.   *MW*

Luca Signorelli
(c. 1445/50 or 1442/43–1523)

192 Portrait of an Elderly Man
c. 1510
Poplar, 50 x 32 cm
Acquired 1894

Luca Signorelli was one of the most
stylistically individual of Raphael's
contemporaries, and within Signorelli's
work this painting is artistically and
iconographically unique. It is not only
the resolute modelling that shows Signorelli's particular qualities: ignoring the
subject-matter and the size of the format
he added some of his characteristic bizarre architecture to the background, as

well as two of his characteristic naked figures, which seem to offer an action study rather than contribute meaning to the painting. To this he added a similar group of figures, giving us a rear-view of a figure leaning on a staff and a recumbent figure which recalls a portrait of the Madonna; his "Pan" is only one of the variants in profile. *MW*

Luca Signorelli
(c. 1445/50 or 1442/43–1523)

193 The Holy Family with Zachariah, Elizabeth and the Boy John,
after 1512
Poplar, diameter 70 cm
Acquired 1875

Two pictures by Signorelli are among the important acquisitions made in the closing years of the 19th century. Signorelli was concerned to deploy human figures within the pictorial space in a precise fashion. The late Berlin tondo is impressive evidence of this. Circular pictures came on the scene in the mid 15th century to early 16th century and there were various ways of handling this difficult format. Signorelli shows himself to be a master of composition here: he not only fits the figures—Joseph with the infant Jesus, Zachariah with the boy John, Mary and Elizabeth—perfectly into the restricting circle, but at the same time they break out of the fictitious space in their lively encounter. Shell shapes are created and emphasised by billowing garments; There is an interplay of limbs and outlines that relate to each other rigorously. Such artistic complexity requires a dark background. The location of the figures can be deduced from the patterned floor. It slopes upwards, showing that the tondo must originally have been hung high. *HN*

The Gemäldegalerie's latest work by Raphael dates from the late Florentine period and shows a marked change vis-à-vis the *Madonna Terranuova*, which dates from only a few years earlier: the palette has become much lighter—even changing from dark to light blonde for the hair—, the chiaroscuro is somewhat more reticent, and the modelling more delicate. The features are softer and fuller, the movements less restrained, livelier and more elegant. Christ is turning his face encouragingly to the viewer in an apparently spontaneous movement. At the same time the horizon is lowered, the landscape becomes more delicate, and the trees more feathery.   *MW*

Raphael   (1483–1520)

194   Madonna Colonna, c. 1508
Poplar, 78.9 x 58.2 cm
Acquired 1827

Raphael   (1483–1520)

195   Madonna Terranuova, c. 1505
Poplar, diameter 88.5 cm
Acquired 1854

This picture was painted shortly after Raphael's arrival in Florence and "was his first attempt at the tondo format that was so popular in that city. The Madonna's face was much more confidently composed than in his three earlier Berlin paintings. Leonardo's influence is becoming stronger than Perugino's. Details like the extreme foreshortening of Mary's hand come from Leonardo, and possibly also the idea of showing the Christ Child with his legs crossed, although this pose could also derive from the Netherlands and a painter like Memling, for example, who is also echoed in the lavish attention paid to the landscape area. Northern aspects of the town featured more conspicuously in the under-drawing. A typically southern feature is the presence of holy children, above all the young John the Baptist.   *MW*

Franciabigio   (1482–1525)

196   Portrait of a Young Man, 1522
Poplar, 78 x 61 cm
Acquired 1829

The shadow over half the face and the deep-set eyes looking thoughtfully into the distance are familiar from Franciabigio's earlier portraits, but the slender proportions and firm, smooth surfaces in the Berlin picture are due to the artist's familiarity with the work of Sebastiano, Andrea del Sarto and Pontormo. The young man's work, defined by the detailed still life in the foreground, suits the meditative mood as do the dark grey clouds, reddening at the horizon. The picture has been identified with a portrait of Matteo Sofferroni mentioned by Vasari, but there is no firm evidence for this. A slip of paper provides the artist's monogram and a precise date.   *MW*

Rosso Fiorentino   (1495–1540)

197   Portrait of a Young Man
Poplar, 82.4 x 59.9 cm
Acquired 1876

The subject poses in front of a landscape background with his body in three-quarter profile and his head turned towards the viewer. In portraits by Sarto and Franciabigio (cf no. 196), there is a balance between the subject and the viewer that is based on mutual benevolence, whereas the young man in Rosso's portrait is eyeing the viewer with a coldly disparaging, insistent look. In this respect Rosso's portrait, which dates from about 1517/18, anticipates later Mannerism.   *SM*

across the block on which the beheaded man's torso is lying. Her provocatively bared breast, her head and the head of John the Baptist form a triangle. This emphasises the destructive and erotic component of the subject matter. Salome's maidservants are standing behind her, and Herod and his retinue are on the right.

The painter Bacchiacca, who worked in Florence and Rome, relates his composition to a woodcut by Dürer dating from 1510. However, the figure of Salome is much more influenced by Michelangelo. *KH*

Bacchiacca (1494–1557)

198 The Beheading of John the Baptist
Poplar, 167 x 149 cm
Acquired 1821

John the Baptist was imprisoned for openly criticising the unlawful marriage of King Herod, Tetrarch of Galilee, to his sister-in-law Herodias. But Herodias's thirst for revenge went further; her daughter Salome was made to dance before Herod and lure him into granting any wish. At her mother's behest she asked for John the Baptist's head on a charger.

The executioner has just done his work. He is handing Salome John's head

Agnolo Bronzino (1503–1572)

199 Ugolino Martelli, 1536/37
Poplar, 102 x 85 cm
Acquired 1878

The turn of the young cleric's body, which is derived from Pontormo, plays off a similar movement in the statue of David in the background. This statue is much larger in its conception and was owned by the Martellis (now in Washington). It is uncertain whether the building-kit architecture, which cramps the figure of Ugolino, does in fact represent the family palace. Writings by Virgil and Homer on the table represent the high points of Latin and Greek verse. Ugolino however is not leaning on these, but on a work by Bembo, who wrote in the "volgare"; thus the subject is taking a position in the bitter language controversies of those years. Contemporaries praised Ugolino's skill in the "three beautiful languages" and in 1537 Aretino included him among Italy's greatest poets. Ugolino was later to lecture frequently on Bembo's sonnets. Bronzino, who himself wrote poems in the vernacular, met Bembo in 1539. The ninth book of the *Iliad* is turned to the viewer and not to Ugolino, which is perhaps intended as an allusion to the superiority of language over brute force. The table ornament is clearly a paraphrase of the Martelli coat of arms. *MW*

Giorgio Vasari (1511–1574)

200 The Apostles Peter and John
Giving a Blessing, 1557
Canvas, 188 x 137 cm
Acquired from the Royal Palaces

The picture comes from a processional
banner painted on both sides that Vasari
painted for the Compagnia dello Spirito
Santo. The miracle of Pentecost was
depicted on the other side. This work
is now in the Bildergalerie in Potsdam-
Sanssouci. The two scenes are closely
linked in terms of content. After the
outpouring of the Holy Spirit at Pentecost, Peter and John appeared together to
spread Christ's teaching as his disciples.
The pentecostal dove hovering over
the scene refers to the divine mission.
The account adds that sick people were
healed by Peter's shadow as he passed
by (Acts of the Apostles 3, 1-10). He is
Christ's representative on earth, is able
to perform miracles and can also be seen
as representing the whole church. The
members of the Brotherhood were iden-
tifying their own discipleship and their
mission to proclaim the gospel in the images on the processional banner that was
carried through the city at Whitsuntide.

Vasari worked as a painter and architect in Arezzo, Florence and Rome.
He travelled a great deal, and collected
material for accounts of Italian artists'
lives, which are important sources of art
history. *KH*

Ferrarese Master

201 Polyhymnia, c. 1455/60
Canvas on poplar, 116.5 x 70.5 cm
Acquired 1894

This picture was painted at the same
time as four other works, which depicted seated Muses (now in Ferrara,
London, Budapest and Milan), for the
Este's studiolo in the Belfiore palace near
Ferrara; four of the panels came from a
single tree-trunk. The damage to all five
pictures could have been caused by a
fire at Belfiore in 1483. The group was

painted under the direction of Tura, and
the Berlin picture stands out because of
its similarity to Piero della Francesca.
The fact that Polyhymnia appears here as
the inventor of agriculture, in the spirit
of the pictorial programme sketched in
1447 by the humanist Guarino, can be
explained by Leonello d'Este's attempts
to introduce agricultural reforms. *MW*

has a contemporary element in the form of a harbour fortification. *HN*

Garofalo (1481?–1559)

203 The Adoration of the Kings
c. 1508/10
Poplar, 70.4 x 83 cm
Acquired 1821

This picture is now generally considered to be a work from the period in which Garofalo was already influenced by Giorgione but not yet by Raphael. It was cleaned in 1988, revealing richly and delicately handled colour that had been hidden by 19th-century over-painting. The landscape area is particularly attractive, and the traditional procession of the Magi is broken down into several groups, and they are garbed with the legendary garment accessories. *MW*

Ercole de' Roberti
(after 1450?–1496)

202 John the Baptist, c. 1480
Poplar, 54 x 31 cm
Acquired 1885

The Ferrara masters Cosmè Tura and Francesco del Cossa had a fundamental effect on Ercole's expressive style. Venetian influences can also be discerned in the landscape here. On the plateau in the foreground the contrapposto figure towers up abruptly—monumentally—in front of the geometrically arranged, horizontally articulated background, which

Lodovico Mazzolino
(1480–1528/30)

204 The Twelve-Year-Old Jesus Teaching in the Temple, 1524
Poplar, 256 x 182.5 cm
Acquired with the Solly Collection, 1821

Christ is arguing with the scribes and Pharisees. Mary and Joseph are approaching from the right, and from the left comes the donor Francesco Caprara in devout attitude. There are people listening on the loggia of the temple in the background. This is decorated on the parapet with monochrome relief scenes inspired by ancient sarcophaguses: on the left they show Judith with the head of Holofernes and the Jews' struggle against the Assyrians, and on the right Goliath struck by the stone from David's sling and the battle against the Philistines. On the rear wall of the temple are two gold reliefs: on the left, Moses with the tablets of the law, and on the right, prophesying the victory of the Jews. The painter worked mainly in Ferrara, but created this altar picture for the Chapel of Francesco Caprara in San Francesco in Bologna.   *KH*

Andrea Mantegna   (1431–1506)

205   Mary with the Sleeping Child
Canvas, 43 x 32 cm
Acquired 1904

Mantegna works with lines that delineate the individual forms distinctly and link mother and child closely together. The picture's intimate, delicate effect derives from the use of thinly applied glue colour. This allows the structure of the canvas to show through clearly and gives the Madonna a look of fragility.   *KH*

and crumpled, fluttering garments suggest emotional excitement. It is unusual in pictures of the Madonna to omit the plinth of the throne, which otherwise raises her considerably, and yet she is the spiritual centre of the spatial composition. Town governor Alessandro Sforza commissioned the altar for the extension to the church of S. Giovanni Battista in Pesaro in up-to-date Renaissance forms; the altar is held to be the first in northern Italy to have a uniform centre panel. Other parts are in Italian and American museums.   *HN*

Marco Zoppo   (1433–1478)

206   Madonna Enthroned with the Child and Saints, 1471
Poplar, 268 x 258 cm
Acquired 1821

The "Sacra Conversazione" seems to be taken unusually literally here: John the Baptist and Jerome are conducting their dispute across the full width of the panel. In the second row St. Paul makes contact with the viewer and seems to draw him into the action. Body movements

Giovanni Bellini   (1430/31–1516)

207   The Dead Christ with Mourning
Angels, c. 1475/80
Poplar, 83 x 67.5 cm
Acquired 1821

Bellini painted even more variations on
the theme of Christ mourned by angels
and/or followers than did his brother-
in-law Mantegna. Probably no-one approached the theme with more profound
religious intensity. The picture achieves a
concentration that is unique in terms of
form and content: the choice of detail is
very tightly restricted and the tomb on
which Jesus is sitting is not visible. Heavy
forms and bodies with a great deal of

three-dimensional modelling combine
very well with confident drawing and
harmoniously lit surfaces to suggest
the middle period of Bellini's creative
activity.   *MW*

Giovanni Bellini   (1430/31–1516)

208   The Resurrection of Christ, 1479
Canvas (transferred from poplar),
148 x 128 cm
Acquired 1903

This picture was intended for Marco
Zorzi's burial chapel in the church of
San Michele in Isola, and this explains
the choice of the resurrection as subject
matter. It is an early and key representative of a group of works in which complex landscapes form a major element. In
this respect Antonello (cf no. 212), who
spent some time in Venice around 1475,
may have had some influence on Bellini,
as he did in encouraging his shift to oil
painting. In this way Bellini was able to
make his work more subtly transparent,
and to convey vividly the transfigured
body of the risen Christ and the delicate
texture of his loincloth.

Unlike most of his contemporaries,
Bellini has the risen Christ float above
the hill in full figure. The accumulated
rock strata call to mind the bleak landscapes of Bellini's earlier work, which
were inspired by his brother-in-law
Mantegna.

The pose and Roman garb of the
two soldiers on the left are also borrowed from Mantegna, while their rather
more everyday companion is reminiscent
of northern art. The nakedness of the
fourth guard is out of place. Bellini was
probably keen to introduce variety and
show off his anatomical knowledge, and
he may also have wanted to provide an
exotic, pagan and ancient touch. Even
amazingly realistic details like the fig
tree or the distant town are rarely an end
in themselves, thus the cormorant may
well stand for death, and the rabbits for
life.   *MW*

Cima da Conegliano
(c. 1459/60–1517/18)

209 The Healing of Anianus,
c. 1497/99
Poplar, 172 x 135 cm
Acquired 1821

This panel is not in very good condition;
additions have been made to the top,
left-hand and bottom edges. The panel
introduced a sequence of four scenes
from the life of St. Mark. The sequence
was set up in the manner of a frieze on
a side wall of the chapel of the Luccan
silk-weavers in Santa Maria dei Crociferi.
Adjacent to this panel was a Sermon of
St. Mark by Lattanzio da Rimini, which
is known only from a preliminary drawing and which would have finished off
the square with architecture arranged in
a kind of mirror-image; another work
from this series, Mansueti's *The Arrest
of St. Mark*, also dated 1499, is in Vaduz.
In this work by Conegliano, Mark, accompanied by a man with a Christ-like
face, is healing the hand of the cobbler
Anianus, who has injured himself with
his awl while mending Mark's shoes
in the marketplace in Alexandria. Four
of the central figures are derived from
a Berlin drawing attributed to Bellini.
The costumes and the gable relief seem
to create an exotic atmosphere, but the
costly marble facing and the Renais-
sance-style capitals, pilaster fillings and
friezes in particular reflect the ideals of
contemporary Venetian architecture. *MW*

Vittore Carpaccio
(1465/67–1525/26)

210   Preparation of Christ's Tomb
c. 1505
Canvas, 145 x 185 cm
Acquired 1905

Carpaccio produced a considerable body
of work, mainly narrative cycles for the
meeting-rooms of Venetian *scuole*, an
example of which in Berlin would be
the *Ordination of Stephen as a Deacon*.
The *Preparation of Christ's Tomb* is one
of his later works, and is very different
from the rest of his oeuvre. The austere
style and the approach to the familiar
theme, equally exceptional in the wealth
of allusions and its gloomy mood, make
the earlier attribution to Mantegna un-
derstandable. The semi-naked old man,
crouching and lost in thought at the foot
of the tree, can be interpreted as Job, the
patient sufferer of the Old Covenant,
humble before his God, and thus a
familiar archetype for the suffering
Christ. At the top left we can make out
the crosses of Golgotha, and on the right
Christ's mourning followers. If the

various man-made objects suggest the
passing of antiquity the Renaissance-
style legs of the table call to mind contemporary forms, and it is a Byzantine
pictorial tradition which places Christ
ceremonially on a table, where his body
can be washed. The anvil-like central
support stands for the red stone of unc-
tion, a highly revered relic in the Orthodox Church. The melancholy calm of
this moment between death and resurrection is underlined by the trumpeter
who is playing in the middle of this
desolate scene. In another altar-panel,
which is now in New York and was
probably painted around 1505–1507,
Carpaccio again placed Job at the side
of the dead Christ. Both paintings were
in the Canonici collection in Ferrara in
1632. Nevertheless, the closely related
theme raises the question of whether,
as has recently been suggested, they
could both actually have been painted
for the Scuola di San Giobbe, which
had been re-established after a move in
1504; other accompanying pieces are so
far unknown, and the Berlin picture is
sometimes dated as late as 1515–1520.

MW

Carlo Crivelli   (1430/35–c. 1495)

211   Madonna with Saints, 1488/89
Poplar, 191 x 196 cm
Acquired 1892

The handing over of the keys to Peter is here joined with the common theme of the enthroned Madonna between standing saints. This is probably the main image for an altar ordered in 1488 for the Franciscan Church of San Pietro degli Osservanti in Camerino. This would explain the honour done to the first Pope and the presence of numerous saints of that order: on the right by the bishop are St. Louis of Toulouse and the blessed Giacomo della Marca, on the left, beside Emidius, the town's patron saint, are the blessed John of Capestrano and St. Francis himself. Crivelli had been away from his home city of Venice for a long time—although he always alluded to it in his signature—working in Dal-matia and the Marches, hence his old-fashioned yet highly individual style. This extends from the use of long-outdated retable forms by way of a delight in exaggeratedly life-like details like the protruding veins right down to the inevitable garlands of carefully painted fruit, which absolutely must include a cucumber. Ornamentally varied fields come together like carpets. The smooth faces with noses bent flat and archaic-looking almond eyes and slightly too sharply drawn, are not fully three-dimensional. Although he abandons the old polyptych format in this late work for the Renaissance pala, this was still enclosed at the sides by pilasters, each with three Gothic-framed figures of saints, one above the other (two of them are now in Berlin).   *MW*

around 1475. This makes the two signed portraits in Berlin all the more significant: one is dated 1474, and the other, his last and smallest one, is dated 1478, that is, long before Bellini took up the Netherlandish manner of abandoning a neutral ground in favour of tree-covered plains. The subject's manner of looking out of the picture is typical of Antonello's portraits, as is the three-quarter view of the subject, which he popularised in Italy.

MW

Antonello da Messina
(c. 1430–1479)

212   Portrait of a Young Man, 1478
Walnut, 20.4 x 14.5 cm
Acquired at the latest 1830

Antonello is the most famous example of the mutual influence of Italian and old Netherlandish painting. There is still just as much controversy about whether he ever crossed the Alps as there is about his concrete relationship with local painting during a nearly two-year stay in Venice

Giorgione   (1477/78–1510)

213   Portrait of a Young Man
Canvas, 58 x 46 cm
Acquired 1891

The subject is shown as a half-length figure against a dark ground, and he turns slightly away from the head-on pose. He is looking coolly and confidently out of the corner of his eye at the viewer, who is kept slightly at a distance by the parapet on which the young man is resting his hand. The portrait's formal regularity and harmony of proportion identify it as a work of the High Renaissance, and make it clearly distinct from Quattrocento portraits. There is controversy about the interpretation of the inscription "V.V." on the parapet as "virtus vincit" or "vivo vivus".

SM

Sebastiano del Piombo
(1485–1547)

214 Portrait of a Young Roman Woman
Poplar, 78 x 61 cm
Acquired 1885

The young woman appears as a half-figure in three-quarter view in front of a window opening onto an evening landscape. With her right hand she is holding the fur-lined velvet cloak which has slipped off her shoulder, and her left hand is resting on a basket of fruit. This is an attribute of St. Dorothy, which may indicate the subject's first name. The portrait is presumed to date from 1513, and shows Raphael's influence. The landscape view is a Venetian motif. *SM*

Palma Vecchio (c. 1480–1528)

215 The Holy Family, c. 1515
Poplar, 61 x 51 cm
Acquired 1815

Following an old standard approach, Palma sets up a contrast between the pensive Joseph and the adoring Mary. He emphasises Mary not merely by size; he shifts the triangle formed by the Holy Family to the left, away from the centre of the picture, emphasising her even more. The framing landscape and the gentle evening light suggest associations with the Rest on the Flight to Egypt. The sketch-like view in the distance, the fine ornamentation on Christ's cushions and clothing and the play of light on Mary's red garments place the picture in the stylistic ambit of the young Titian and Giorgione, but Mary's broad, bulky proportions are typical features of Palma's work. *MW*

Lorenzo Lotto (c. 1480–1556)

216 Christ's Farewell to his Mother, 1521
Canvas, 126 x 99 cm
Acquired 1821

Christ, accompanied by Peter and Thomas (?), is saying goodbye to his mother in an open, barrel-vaulted columned hall, with a view through the arches into a landscape and garden. After telling her about the sufferings he will have to face, he kneels and asks for her blessing. The Madonna is caught by Mary Magdalene and John as she collapses to the ground. The picture was painted in Bergamo in 1521 and according to Ridolfi (1648) was originally in the house of Domenico Tassi. The donor represented on the right is probably Elisabetta Rota, Tassi's wife. He was portrayed on a lost companion piece, depicting the Adoration of the Child. *SM*

Paris Bordon (1500–1571)

217 Two Chess Players, c. 1540
Canvas, 116 x 184.5 cm
Acquired from the Royal Palaces

Two Venetian noblemen are playing chess against the backdrop of the terraces and gardens of a Renaissance villa. The player on the right is in the act of checkmating his opponent; both are looking at the viewer.

The game of chess takes on something of the role of an attribute in this double portrait of a prestigious nature. It is a sign of intellectual education and a refined way of living. The extravagance of this refined lifestyle is made clear by

the guinea-fowl at the front of the terrace, which has been imported from Africa as a pet.

Other pastimes of contemporary "villeggiatura", the noble villa existence of the age, are shown: card games, a picnic in the park and the lively conversation in which two gentlemen are immersed outside the colonnade. The youth with a falcon behind them may be a reference to the pleasures of hunting. 		*KH*

Titian (1488/90–1576)

218 Portrait of Clarissa Strozzi at the Age of Two, 1542
Canvas, 115 x 98 cm
Acquired 1878

Clarissa Strozzi was the daughter of Roberto Strozzi and Magdalena de' Medici of Florence, who were in exile in Venice from 1536 to 1542. The two-year-old girl is richly adorned and stands in a white silk dress by a stone table, feeding her little dog a pretzel. Despite this apparently playful pose the little figure positively exudes steadfastness and dignity. Titian's portrait of Clara Strozzi is one of the earliest portraits of a child in Italian painting. 		*SM*

Titian (1488/90–1576)

219 Venus with the Organ Player,
c. 1550/52
Canvas, 115 x 210 cm
Acquired 1918

Venus, accompanied by Cupid, is lying
on a ceremonial couch in an open loggia. Her slightly raised torso is set against
the background of a red velvet curtain,
which covers the right upper third of the
picture and opens up a view of an extensive landscape in the centre. On the left,
at the foot of the couch, a well-dressed
cavalier is sitting in front of the organ;
his hands are on the keyboard but he has
eyes only for the goddess's bare beauty.
The unusual combination of Venus and
organ player, which exists in a few other
variations, is an iconographic innovation
by Titian.

There are contradictory hypotheses
about the origins and interpretation of
the painting: some say that the picture
follows neo-Platonic ideas by symboli-
cally representing the senses of seeing
and hearing as they recognise beauty.
But this is countered by the notion that
the nude female figure is a lady or courtesan who is being wooed by the organ-
ist with the aid of his music, with Cupid
interpreted as the cavalier's messenger of
love.   *SM*

Jacopo Tintoretto (1518–1594)

220 Mary with the Child,
Venerated by Two Evangelists
Canvas, 228 x 160 cm
Acquired 1841

This altar-piece dating from c. 1570/75
was painted by Tintoretto alone, without
assistance from his studio. The depiction
of Mary with a crown of stars above the
sickle moon as the Woman of the Apocalypse and Immaculata, appearing to the
Evangelists as if in a vision, is typical of
Counter-Reformation veneration of
Mary.   *SM*

Veronese (1528–1588)

221 The Dead Christ, Supported by Two Mourning Angels, before 1588
Canvas, 110 x 94 cm
Acquired 1815

The pictorial type featuring a Pietà with angels emerged in France around 1400. In Venice, Giovanni Bellini depicted the subject several times and developed it further as an independent devotional picture. There is an example dating from 1480/85 in the Gemäldegalerie. Veronese's version dates from about 100 years later.

The greenish-grey body of the dead Christ stands in stark contrast with the angels' fair curls. The angel on the left is showing Christ's hand with the stigmata. Christ is dead, yet it seems as though the

second angel is speaking to him; his head is very close to that of the dead Christ, and his hand is pointing to the viewer in a gesture that suggests speaking. Indeed, Christ's mouth and eyes are open. The marked sensuality of this portrayal, the dead Christ's physicality (note the veins and muscles in his arms), supported by the colour and the chiaroscuro, are all aimed to attract the viewer's sympathy and anticipate principles of Baroque painting. *KH*

Girolamo Romanino
(1484/87–1559)

222 Salome with the Head of John the Baptist, c. 1516/17
Poplar, 86 x 71.5 cm
Acquired 1821

Romanino's Salome follows a pictorial type that emerged in northern Italy in the 16th century: reflection about what has happened. Salome radiates eroticism, with full lips, loose hair and a dreamy expression. Behind her there is a servant girl on the left and the executioner on the right. *KH*

Savoldo (c. 1480/85–after 1548)

223 The Venetian Woman (St. Mary Magdalene), c. 1535/40
Canvas, 92 x 73 cm
Acquired 1821

Earlier versions of this work in London, Florence (Pitti Palace) and Zurich (private collection) depict a vessel of ointment before the open tomb in the bottom left-hand corner, rather than a signature. This attribute of Mary Magdalene is missing in the Berlin painting; thus the subject's identity is deliberately ambiguous. What we see, then, is a bewildering game played with the veiled face of the woman, whose image is powerfully highlighted by the light and gold of her garments. The wall further increases her dominance of the picture, as it does not allow the viewer's eye to escape. In the London picture the fabric has a silver sheen—perhaps as a reflection of the risen Christ. The dense surface of the Berlin painting almost suggests metal foil.   *MW*

Moretto   (c. 1498–1554)

224   The Adoration of the Shepherds
c. 1540/45
Canvas, 402 x 273 cm
Acquired 1841

This late high-altar panel, signed bottom left, is by far the largest picture in the Gemäldegalerie. A companion piece dated 1541 from the same church, S. Maria della Ghiaia in Verona, has been missing since 1945. The format is just as typical of Moretto's work as the massive figures, towering up at the very front of the picture, and sometimes slightly distorted. Behind this rises, in Moretto's much-praised silvery light, a setting that allows only narrow views out to the side, partly a stable, and partly a symbol of the victory over paganism: in the niche and behind the shepherds front left are fragments of an image of a naked god.   *MW*

Giovanni Battista Moroni
(1520/24–1578)

225   Don Gabriel de la Cueva, Duke of Alburquerque
Canvas, 114.5 x 90.8 cm
Acquired 1979

Moroni's picture of the Duke of Alburquerque dates from the time when Lombardy was under Spanish rule. The subject had been the governor of Milan since 1564. He is posing calmly and unapproachably in front of almost abstract-looking architecture. His hand resting on the plinth draws attention to his motto: "Here I stand without fear, and death holds no terrors for me."   *SM*

Giovanni Antonio Boltraffio and Marco d'Oggiono
(1467–1516 / 1467–1524)

226 The Resurrection of Christ
with SS. Leonard of Noblac and Lucia
1491/94
Poplar, 234.5 x 185.5 cm
Acquired 1821

This picture is by painters from Leonardo's circle of pupils. Boltraffio was responsible for Christ's robe and the figures of the two saints, and Marco d'Oggiono painted Christ's head and arms and the landscape in the back-ground. The altarpiece was created for the Chapel of St. Leonard near S. Giovanni sul Muro in Milan. The chapel was endowed in 1484 by Leonardo Griffi, the Archbishop of Benevento, and built by his heirs, who also commissioned the artists concerned.

The witnesses of Christ's resurrection are two saints. St. Leonard (c. 500–570) was Leonardo Griffi's patron saint, and abbot of the Benedictine monastery of Noblac, which the saint had founded. As the patron saint of prisoners he has a hand restraint at his feet. Lucia of Syracuse (d. 310 during the persecution of the Christians) is said to have sent her eyes to her sceptical bridegroom, and in return for this received more beautiful ones from the Madonna.   KH

Francesco Melzi   (1493–c. 1570)

227   Vertumnus and Pomona
c. 1518/22
Poplar wood, 186 x 135.5 cm
Acquired from the Royal Palaces

The tree-nymph Pomona was worshipped in Latium as the goddess of orchards. Vertumnus, a god of vegetation and the seasons, had the ability to change his shape. He approached Pomona in the form of an old woman. In her garden there was an elm tree with a vine growing around its trunk. The old woman interpreted this as a symbol of marital union. The old woman sang Vertumnus's praises as the only possible spouse, and told her various cautionary tales. Finally, Vertumnus returned to his true form. His good looks ultimately won Pomona over, and she agreed to become his wife (Ovid, *Metamorphoses*).

As a young man Francesco Melzi met Leonardo da Vinci. He went with him to Rome in 1513, to France and, sometime before 1517, to the court of François I. Leonardo left him his artistic estate. The figure of Pomona is derived from the Mary in Leonardo da Vinci's cartoon of St. Anne (London, Royal Academy).   KH

Prospero Fontana   (1512–1597)

228   The Adoration of the Kings
c. 1548/50
Poplar, 318.5 x 186.5 cm
Acquired 1821

The Adoration of the Kings is presented as a spectacle, involving a large number of human figures and animals, not as an event to be contemplated. The great range of expressive gestures is a striking feature; directly behind the richly adorned black king, a horse is rearing up. Fontana was one of the principal exponents of Bolognese Mannerism. This altarpiece was commissioned by Lucio Maggi for his family chapel in the Church of S. Maria delle Grazie in Bologna, which no longer exists. Fontana drew upon Vasari's 1547/48 altarpiece in S. Fortunato in Rimini.   KH

Correggio   (c. 1489–1534)

229   Leda and the Swan, c. 1531/32
Canvas, 152 x 191 cm
Acquired 1829

This picture was part of a cycle depicting
Jupiter's amorous adventures in various
guises, which Correggio painted for the
Duke of Mantua, Federico II Gonzaga,
c. 1530/32.

Leda, the principal figure in the Berlin picture, was the daughter of the King
of Aetolia, and married to the Spartan
King Tyndareus. Correggio painted the
commonest of the various versions of the
ancient myth: Jupiter approached Leda
on the banks of the river Eurota in the
guise of a swan and seduced her. Leda
and the swan can be seen on the bank in
front of a clump of trees, on the left are
two amoretti with wind instruments and
a boyish Cupid with his lyre. It is uncertain whether the figures on the right are
Leda's companions or a simultaneous
presentation of other scenes from the
story. Three other pictures from the cycle
have survived as well as the *Leda*: the
painting of the *Danäe* in Rome, and

also the *Abduction of Ganymede* and *Io*,
both in Vienna. Egon Verheyen has
suggested that the pictures were intended
to decorate a hall in the Palazzo del Tè,
the Duke's summer residence. The hall
was part of an "appartamento" that may
have been intended for Isabella Boschetti,
the Duke's official mistress.

The cycle found its way to Spain and
into the possession of Philip II, presumably after the death of Federico II. The
Berlin picture passed through famous
collections in the course of the 16th and
17th centuries and came into the possession of Philippe of Orléans, the Regent
of France, in 1721. His son Louis found
the portrayal of Leda offensive, and cut
the painting to pieces in an attack of
religious frenzy, destroying the head of
Leda. The painter Coypel put it together
again and filled in the missing pieces.
Frederick the Great acquired the picture
for his gallery in Sanssouci in 1755. Jacob
Schlesinger repainted Leda's head when
the painting moved to the Museum am
Lustgarten in 1830.   *SM*

Ludovico Carracci (1555–1619)

230 Christ in the Wilderness, Served
by Angels, c. 1608/10
Canvas, 157.2 x 225.3 cm
Acquired 1985

Religious subjects dominate Ludovico's
oeuvre. He went beyond Mannerism
and, as the first exponent of Baroque
painting in the Bologna area, prepared
the way for Guido Reni and Guercino.
The Berlin picture was painted during
the period of transition to his late style.
As frequently happens in the work of
Carracci, the figures are kept relatively
small in relation to the overall area, while
great importance is given to the landscape. The light, which allows the unusual local colours to shine out directly
over broad areas of the picture, is familiar
from other works by Carracci, and so is
the romantic, fantastic night atmosphere,
which makes the painting seem strangely
modern. The figures of the angels, delicately elongated and standing out effectively against the dark forest ground, also
contribute to the eerie atmosphere; they
have faces typical of Ludovico's style,
with over-large eyes, long, narrow noses
and low brows. An unusual number of
them are trying to help the Messiah, who

is at the beginning of his public mission;
he has just resisted the temptations of the
Devil, who is disappearing into the sky at
the top left. Careful examination reveals
even more angels, including the ghostly
shadowy figures in the clouds, which are
bathed in pallid light—approximately
two dozen in all. Some are bringing fresh
food on a covered plate, while others are
already cleaning the tableware. Others
again are playing musical instruments.
But the four in the main group are
exclusively concerned with solemnly
washing Christ's hands like a priest before the consecration—a new feature for
this theme that was much used at the
time, although it was often precisely the
liturgical associations that determined
this choice. For this reason the table,
sparsely equipped as an altar, does not
seem so out of place. It was scarcely
suitable as an altar-piece because of its
horizontal format, and it found its way
into a Bolognese collection as early as
1678.   *MW*

Successor of Annibale Carracci
(1560–1609)

231 River Landscape with Fortress
and Bridge, c. 1600
Canvas, 73 x 143 cm
Acquired 1815

This river landscape was in the possession of Marquis Vincenzo Giustiniani in
Rome before 1637. A fortress towering
up in the middle of the picture gives
the pictorial space a central axis and
divides two landscape views. The bridge
and fortress are unmistakably inspired
by the Ponte Fabricio in Rome and the
Tiber island. Despite the strong overall
structure and the symmetrical approach
the landscape does not look over-com-
posed, but like a detail from nature. This
average-quality painting, together with

the *Landscape with the Rest on the Flight
into Egypt*, painted by the artist around
1603/04, is a remarkable example of
classical Roman landscape painting. It
had a major influence on Carracci's pupil
Domenichino, and also on Nicolas Poussin and Claude Lorrain.   *SM*

Guercino   (1591–1666)

232 The Betrothal of St. Catherine
1620
Canvas, 88 x 70 cm
Acquired 1970

Typical of Guercino's early, pre-Roman
phase are the very delicate gradations of
the main sections, shimmering as if they
were wet in contrast with the heavily
applied paint in the garments, fur and
jewellery, and the pallid ground tone,
which makes the little red and blue that
is caught by the light glow all the more
warmly. The subject is the frequently
reproduced mystical marriage of
St. Catherine with the infant Jesus.
Here he is still clasping the ring to his
chest, while Mary lifts up the saint's ring
finger. The varied gazes and subtle handling of light create powerful diagonals
over the space—effects that Guercino
developed more clearly here than in the
preliminary drawing (Oxford).   *MW*

Caravaggio (1571–1610)

233 Cupid as Victor, 1601/02
Canvas, 156 x 113 cm
Acquired 1815

The young Cupid, following Virgil's saying "Amor vincit omnia" (Love conquers all), triumphs over science, art, fame and power, whose symbols are strewn at his feet: musical instruments, straight-edge, laurel wreath, and pieces of armour. The boy's ambiguous mocking smile and the provocatively importunate pose suggest that earthly love is mocking the highest moral and intellectual values of human ambition. The boy's precarious position, with his left leg on the edge of a draped bed, so that his genitals thrust almost into the centre of the picture, strikes a homoerotic note. The chiaroscuro and the incredibly natural quality of the figures are typical of Caravaggio.

SM

Giovanni Baglione
(1573–1644)

234 The Divine Eros Defeats the
Earthly Eros, c. 1602/03
Canvas, 183.4 x 121.4 cm
Acquired 1815

Baglione's Eros for Cardinal Benedetto
Giustiniani (1544–1621) was a response
to the Eros that Caravaggio had painted
for Marchese Vincenzo Giustiniani
(1564–1637), the Cardinal's brother.
Caravaggio had drawn a pretty, provocatively naked boy as a youthful god of
earthly love to be a victor over the "liberal arts", power and fame. As well as this
he gave him the features of a boy who
had also been a model for religious
figures. This was a challenge to his
contemporaries' moral values.

   Baglione has Earthly Love thrown to
the ground by a divine Eros in armour.
A devil with faun's ears and a trident is
crouching bottom left. Antiquity was
well aware of the competition between
Eros and Anteros for the soul of man. If
the two are reconciled, then perfect love
is achieved.

   In contrast with this, Baglione's picture, according to the official church
teaching of his time, aims at the subju-
gation of earthly love. The divine Eros,

reminiscent of the falling St. Michael, is
drawing back his arm for the final thrust.

KH

Orazio Gentileschi (1563–1639)

235 David with the Head of Goliath,
c. 1610
Copper, 36.7 x 28.7 cm
Acquired 1914. Property of the
Kaiser Friedrich-Museums-Verein

David is standing over Goliath's head
with his sword in his hand, and is sunk
deep in contemplation. Behind him is a
rocky grotto beyond which is a landscape
view. His reflective mood is an iconographic innovation to the extent that
previously artists showed either David
as he cut off Goliath's head or David
in triumph with the severed head. The
picture dates from 1610 and is a variation
on a larger picture on canvas in the Gal-
leria Spada in Rome. Gentileschi is the
most important and the most independent of the Roman painters influenced
by Caravaggio. This can be seen in the
naturalistic treatment of the figure, but
the emphasised landscape elements and
the choice of a small format are probably
due to Elsheimer.

SM

Bernardo Strozzi (1581–1644)

236 Salome, after 1630
Canvas, 124 x 94 cm
Acquired 1914. Property of the
Kaiser Friedrich-Museums-Verein

Strozzi, more than any other artist affected by Flemish art, seems to have become a legend in his lifetime as the epitome of natural talent. After ten years in a Capuchin monastery in his home town of Genoa he was given leave in 1608 to look after his mother. After she died he spent the last eleven years of his life in Venice, where he was greatly admired, as a fugitive from his order. Despite the extravagance of the thickly applied paint, the Berlin picture, with the half-length format so favoured by the painter, gives a good impression of his masterly handling of materials and colour. The lively line of the very broad brush can be traced everywhere. In order to create special effects, the ground was worked while it was still wet, and this is evident not least in the cords of the doublet. The virtuoso tendency towards the abstract reaches its climax in the servant-girl's neckline: scarcely any form, just layers of glowing colour. Salome is grabbing hold of a lock of John the Baptist's hair almost mischievously. Her lively face with Strozzi's typically rosy cheeks shows scarcely any sense of horror. *MW*

er's eye moves from the squire, who has his back to us, over the shifting silhouette of Alexander, which is almost entirely in shadow, to the over-large figure of the philosopher, who is preaching the simple life and living in a barrel. His gesture suggests that he is asking the ruler of the world for absolutely nothing more than to stop blocking the sunlight from him—even though it is shining directly on his face alone, and making the materials, with their thickly applied paint and lively brushwork, glow so very intensely. *MW*

Gioacchino Assereto (1600–1649)

237 Alexander and Diogenes
c. 1625/35
Canvas, 180 x 148 cm
Acquired 1984

This picture marks a high point in the oeuvre of this leading exponent of Genoese Baroque. It dates from the phase around 1630, which was distinguished by great subtlety of colour due to the black underpainting. The squire, who is not essential to the action, deftly extends the pictorial structure, some of which was developed only when it was being painted, into a group of three: the view-

Carlo Dolci (1616–1686)

238 St. John the Evangelist, c. 1635/40
Canvas, 115.2 x 93.7 cm
Acquired from the Royal Palaces

Dolci was one of the most important
Florentine painters of the 17th century.
Characteristic features are his refined
painting technique, combined with powerful local colouring, and the intensely
religious expressive quality of his figures.
The observer is challenged to share the
experience of the pictorial subject. St.
John the Evangelist, with his attributes
of eagle, book and writing utensils, has
been banished to the island of Patmos,
where he is writing Revelation. He is
seen from below, in a moment of divine
inspiration. His eyes are turned upward
to heaven, his lips are open and his head
is surrounded by a corona. The painting
is possibly part of a series of octagonal
depictions of the Evangelists. An inscription on the reverse reveals that it was a
gift to King Friedrich Wilhelm I in
1818.   *KH*

Giuseppe Maria Crespi
(1665–1747)

239 The Birth of Arcas or The Birth
of Adonis(?), c. 1720/25
Canvas, 94 x 74 cm
Acquired 1968

Five female figures are portrayed, against
a background of a landscape with a
farmstead. The principal figure is resting
in the left foreground. She is holding a
staff with her right arm. Bow and quiver
are on the ground. To her right, two
companions are keeping a look-out. In
the front a woman or nurse is soothing
the new-born child.

Two interpretations of the scene are
suggested: the birth of Arcas to Callisto
or the birth of Adonis to Myrrha (Ovid,
Metamorphoses). The nymph Callisto,
who was seduced by Jupiter in the
form of the goddess Diana, has fled to
the woods and given birth to Arcas, the
future founder of Arcadia. No other
picture of this episode has survived.
Callisto had been turned into a she-
bear by Diana, and as an outlaw would
be unlikely to have been allowed other
nymphs as servants.

On the birth of Adonis: Cinyras had
unwittingly seduced his own daughter
Myrrha. The pregnant woman was transformed into a myrrh tree, from whose
bursting bark the new-born Adonis
was taken with Diana as midwife, and
brought up by mountain nymphs. This
interpretation is unlikely in the absence
of a myrrh tree. The question of subject
must remain unresolved.   *KH*

Luca Giordano (1634–1705)

240 St. Michael, c. 1663
Canvas, 198 x 147 cm
Acquired 1971. Property of the
Kaiser Friedrich-Museums-Verein

The story of the Archangel Michael's
victory over Satan and the renegade
angels is told in Revelation (12, 7-9).
As a Christian knight, St. Michael was
perceived as a symbol of the Catholic
Church victorious over Protestantism
and the Turkish threat. In Giordano's
version the brightly glowing colour and
the powerfully thrusting figure of the
angel underline the triumphal nature
of the scene. The picture was originally
intended for an altar, but it is not known
for which church. It was painted c. 1663,
and is part of a phase in Giordano's
output in which he was influenced by
the Bolognese painter Guido Reni. His
model was Reni's altar panel dating from
shortly before 1636 in the Capuchin
church in Rome. Giordano was also
aware, from engravings, of Raphael's
St. Michael (1518). Satan's grotesque face
was based on an etching by the Neapolitan Jusepe de Ribera (1591–1652).   *KH*

Francesco Solimena (1657–1747)

241 Madonna of the Rosary
Canvas, 247 x 168 cm
Acquired 1971

This work, painted by Solimena in his youth, was an altar-piece for a chapel of the rosary in the church of a Dominican monastery. He adopted the Roman manner of depiction, in which the number of saints is limited to two (St. Dominic and St. Catharine of Siena). It remains a matter of speculation whether this Berlin painting is the one in Sessa Aurunca mentioned by Solimena's biographer De Dominici (1743).

An X-ray of the Berlin picture reveals two figures of angels at the top in the style of Pietro da Cortona, which Solimena removed in the final version, probably for the sake of the composition. The golden-green cloth remains from the robe of the angel on the left. He filled the empty spaces thus created in the sky with the heads of cherubs.

New clues to its origin are given by the copy recently discovered in Casali di Roccapiemonte and dated 1771. There the figures of angels, which were presumably not painted over until the 19th century, have been retained.   *RC*

Francesco de Mura (1696–1782)

242 Procession of Bacchus, c. 1760
Canvas, 77 x 115 cm
Acquired 1924

The *Procession of Bacchus* must have been painted as part of an interior decor. Bacchus, god of wine and fertility, appears in a triumphal chariot drawn by panthers, accompanied by nymphs and satyrs and followed by the drunken Silenus on a donkey. The large number of elegantly agile figures evokes the great tradition of Neapolitan Baroque painting, but de Mura's light, sometimes

cool colouring already anticipates Neo-Classicism.   *SM*

Jacopo Amigoni   (1682–1752)

243   Abraham Sacrifices Isaac
Canvas, 115 x 150 cm
Loaned by the Streit Foundation, Berlin

As part of a series based on four Old
Testament stories, this impressive picture
is presumed to have been painted between 1739 and 1747, when the much-
travelled painter spent an extended
period in Venice. The four paintings
came to Berlin in the 18th century as
part of the Streit Foundation (cf no. 248).
Atypical for Amigoni, this highly emotional scene is based on 17th-century
models.   *SM*

Marco Ricci   (1676–1730)

244   Southern Landscape in the
Evening Light, c. 1720
Canvas, 94.3 x 108 cm
Acquired 1975

Marco Ricci revealed the achievements
of his Neapolitan, Roman and Genoese predecessors to Venice. He was first
influenced by painters of the "fantastic"
(Magnasco, Peruzzini), then later by
the classical tendency and the northern
Italianists. In the Berlin picture, under
which even the naked eye can see traces
of an earlier work, he achieved a particularly calm composition in bright, warm
colours. The romantic and playful tree-
tops guide the eye, in subtle backlighting,
past southern-looking buildings into the
distance, right down to the faraway bay.
The scattered genre motifs relate to the
evening mood   *MW*

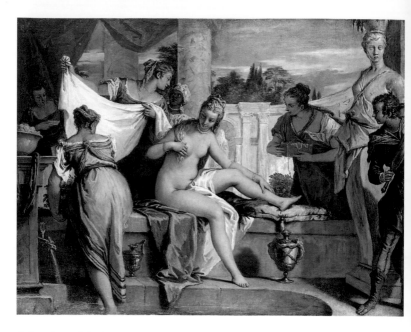

Sebastiano Ricci (1659–1734)

245 Bathsheba Bathing
Canvas, 111.8 x 144.3 cm
Acquired from the Royal Palaces

Ricci's *Bathsheba Bathing* was painted in
1725, in the artist's late period, when he
was moving strongly towards the style of
Veronese. From the palace's battlements,
King David observes Bathsheba, wife
of the soldier Urias, while she is taking
a bath. He sent messengers to summon
her, and committed adultery. When she
became pregnant he contrived that her
husband should be killed in battle and
married her. The moralising aspects that
were still attached to the theme until the
16th century were suppressed in Ricci's
picture in favour of an erotic presentation of female beauty. In fact people very
quickly forgot that the picture was telling the story of Bathsheba, and for a long
time it was entitled "Toilet of Venus" or
"After the Bath". It was only the figure
of the female messenger on the left-hand
edge of the picture that made the correct
interpretation possible. Ricci invokes his
model, Veronese, in his rendering of the
figures and use of sumptuous, silvery-
cool tones for the colour of the clothes.

The setting, a Venetian Renaissance villa,
also features frequently in Veronese's
work. It is therefore not surprising that
Frederick the Great bought the picture
as a supposed Veronese; the misattribu-
tion was not corrected until 1909.   *SM*

Giovanni Battista Tiepolo
(1696–1770)

246 The Martyrdom of St. Agatha
c. 1755
Canvas, 184 x 131 cm
Acquired 1878

Tiepolo painted St. Agatha's martyrdom,
one of his most important altarpieces,
for the high altar of the Benedictine
convent church of S. Agata in Lendinara
near Rovigo. St. Agatha was martyred in
Catania in 251. After she had been ar-
rested and tortured, the executioner cut
off her breasts, but St. Peter appeared to
her in the dungeon and healed her. During another session of torture, part of the
building collapsed and buried two executioners, and there was an earthquake
in Catania. After giving thanks to God
for having survived her torture, the saint
finally died. In the early Baroque pe-

riod artists preferred to show her being healed by St. Peter, but Tiepolo presents her martyrdom. She has collapsed on the steps of an ancient building, looking humbly upwards, while a maidservant covers her mutilated chest with a cloth. A youth on the left is carrying the severed breasts away on a tray, and the threatening figure of the hangman towers on the right. Tiepolo has depicted the moment after the martyrdom, and thus avoided gory explicitness. The principal figure is singled out by the light colours of the flesh-tones and her garment, and conveys an impression of calm trust in God and strength of faith. As we see from an etching by Giandomenico Tiepolo after his father's picture, the painting was originally semicircular at the top. The saint's vision could be seen in the clouds above her, that of the blazing heart of Christ surrounded by the crown of thorns, with the heads of two angels.

SM

Giovanni Battista Tiepolo
(1696–1770)

247 Rinaldo and Armida
in Armida's Magic Garden
Canvas, 39 x 62.4 cm
Acquired 1908; 2000

Tiepolo probably painted two larger
pictures of scenes from Tasso's *Gerusa-
lemme Liberata* with the same themes as
the Berlin pictures for Würzburg in 1753.
We do not know whether the latter were
preparatory sketches or smaller repeated
versions. The first picture shows the
knight Rinaldo succumbing to the spell
of the magician Armida. The knights
Carlo and Ubaldo are approaching in the
background. They have set off from the
Crusaders' camp to look for him. In the
second scene Carlo and Ubaldo are drag-
ging Rinaldo away from Armida to take
him back to the Crusader army. *SM*

Canaletto (1697–1768)

248 Il Campo di Rialto
Canvas, 119 x 186 cm
Loan from the Streit Foundation, Berlin

This view of the main commercial centre in Venice was commissioned by the
Berlin merchant Sigismund Streit, who
was living in Venice. Canaletto painted
the view of the Grand Canal with the
Palazzo Foscari, in which Streit was
living, at the same time. Streit wanted to
preserve his private and professional life
for posterity in these pictures, when he
presented these and two other works by
Canaletto to his old school, the Gymna-
sium zum Grauen Kloster in Berlin, in
1763 as part of a foundation grant. All
four of these paintings are now in the
Gemäldegalerie. *SM*

Francesco Guardi   (1712–1793)

249   The Ascent by Balloon, 1784
Canvas, 66 x 51 cm
Acquired 1901. Property of the Kaiser
Friedrich-Museums-Verein

The first balloon ascent in Venice, which
is depicted here, took place in 1784 from
St. Mark's, but Guardi chose to transfer
it to the entrance of the Giudecca canal. Numerous spectators are watching
the event from the shady portico of the
customs house. The particular charm of
the picture lies not least in the contrast
between the dark frame provided by the
portico and the light, blue sky.   *SM*

Giovanni Paolo Panini
(1691–1765)

250   The Duc de Choiseul Departs
from St. Peter's Square in Rome, 1754
Canvas, 152 x 195 cm
Acquired 1980

The Duc de Choiseul, French ambassador to the Holy See, is shown returning
from his audience with Pope Benedict

XIV against the magnificent backdrop
of St. Peter's Square in Rome. The way
in which the light and the figures are
depicted draws the viewer's eye to the
ambassador's magnificent coach. Choiseul lived in Rome from 1747 to 1757
and commissioned the painting himself,
which combines a commemorative scene
with vedute.   *SM*

Pompeo Batoni   (1708–1787)

251   The Marriage of Cupid and
Psyche
Canvas, 85 x 120.5 cm
Acquired from the Royal Palaces, 1829

Apuleius's narrative tells us that the
marriage of Cupid and Psyche became
possible only after a long series of trials.
Cupid, led by Hymen, the god of wed-
dings, is putting the ring on Psyche's
finger.

On the left sits Venus, Cupid's mother,
in a chariot drawn by doves. Sitting on a
cloud to the right is Zephyr, who helped
the lovers in the story. Next to him the
eye is directed towards a terrace revealing
a hilly landscape.

The picture came from the collection
of Frederick the Great, who commissioned it from Batoni in Rome in 1756.
The high esteem that this painter enjoyed with the king can be seen from the
fact that Frederick kept the painting with
him throughout the Seven Years' War
(1756–1763), and finally chose it as the
only work by a contemporary painter for
his picture gallery in Sanssouci. The king
later failed to secure Batoni's services as
court painter in Sanssouci. With Mengs,

Batoni was the most celebrated painter
in 18th-century Rome.

He painted religious pictures, mythological and allegorical scenes and also a
large number of outstanding portraits,
especially of English visitors to Rome,
which were to a large extent the basis of
his fame.

Batoni can be identified as the artist
who perfected Roman Baroque painting;
but his style, based on that of Raphael
and ancient models, points beyond this,
and makes him one of the forerunners of
Neo-Classicism.   *SM*

Hans Rottenhammer   (1564–1625)

252   The Allegory of the Arts
c. 1600
Copper, 28 x 22.3 cm
Acquired from the Royal Palaces, 1829

Personifications of painting (centre),
architecture (left), poetry (front left)
and music (front right), protected by
Minerva, who can be seen in the background on the left, are striving to be
recognised by Venus, the legendary
incarnation of beauty. While Cupid is
crowning the head of Venus, "painting",

placed almost centrally in the picture, is being strikingly chosen as victor. Thus the sister arts are being subordinated to her. Consequently their future duty will be to support "painting" in praising beauty. This little panel painted by Rottenhammer in Venice is appealing in its almost old-master-like colouring. The influence of landscape painting by Jan Brueghel the Elder, whom Rottenhammer met in Venice, can also be seen here. His artistic virtuosity and the usually small format of his pictures made them popular for princely art collections. Frederick the Great bought the Berlin painting, through an agent, at an auction in Amsterdam in 1771.   *RM*

Adam Elsheimer   (1578–1610)

253   The Holy Family with the Boy John and Angels, c. 1599
Copper, 37.5 x 24.3 cm
Acquired 1928

The Frankfurt painter left his home town in 1598. On his way to Italy he passed some time in the Munich area. Elsheimer probably crossed the Alps for Venice in 1599. Dürer had taken the same route, through Tyrol and the Veneto, over two generations earlier. Elsheimer had already studied his work in some detail. The painter brought two legend-

ary events together in the little Berlin copper panel: "The Rest on the Flight to Egypt" and the caressing "Christ Child Meeting the Boy John" after his return. In this picture, Mary sits beneath a palm tree and on her lap is the Christ Child, who is playfully reaching toward the nearby John.

On the left, the Lamb of God with the stem of the cross (John the Baptist's attribute) can be made out, and on the right Joseph the carpenter with his axe. Garlanded angels of various "ages" are singing their praises and filling up the space. The fantasy landscape is bathed in silvery light.

The quasi-old-master style of the composition is reminiscent of the painting of the Danube school (such as Albrecht Altdorfer, Lucas Cranach the Elder, and Wolf Huber), which flourished just under a century before. The painting probably originated in Venice, and could have been used for the devotions of a patron with traditional tastes in art.   *RM*

Johann Liss (c. 1597–1631)

254 The Ecstasy of St. Paul c. 1628/29
Canvas, 80 x 58.5 cm
Acquired 1919

The painting shows a heavenly vision of
which we have an indirect account from
Paul in 2 Corinthians (12, 1-4). Liss came
from Oldenburg in Holstein, but worked
mainly in Venice. Our picture was probably painted here. Paul falls abruptly
back into the enclosure, surprised by the
sudden burst of the music of the spheres
from the angels, who dissolve in light
and colour. The fragments of colour,
characterised by differently heightened
white and changing formats, make a crucial contribution to the "vitality" of the
Baroque composition. An engraved reproduction by the Amsterdam publisher
Nicolas Visscher (1618–1709) confirms
the authorship and subject of the Berlin
picture.   *RM*

Johann Heinrich Schönfeld
(1609–1684)

255 The Triumph of Venus
c. 1640/45
Canvas, 70 x 123.7 cm
Acquired 1925. Property of the
Kaiser Friedrich-Museums-Verein

A triumphal carriage with a sacrificial
altar is following Mercury and Hercules.
It is unusual in art south of the Alps for
a procession to describe a curve, a treatment reminiscent of Dutch models
(H. van Balen or J. Brueghel the Elder).
The painting appeals because of its gra-
cious figures, the intricacy of the architectural drawing and the relatively light
colouring. In this way the composition,
despite its rich colour contrasts, already
indicates characteristic features of Rococo style. The picture was painted in
Naples, where Schönfeld was presumably
stimulated by magnificent processions
with fantastic effects at the court of the
Spanish viceroys.   *RM*

Sebastian Stoskopff   (1597–1657)

256   Still Life with Glasses and Bottles
1641/44
Canvas, 124.8 x 101.5 cm
Acquired 1973

This Alsatian painter lived in Paris from
about 1622 to 1639. This work gives a
good impression of a neglected genre: an
impressive still life is presented on choice
table linen against a dark background.
The composition is dominated by the
rectangular basket with sparkling glasses.
Three wine bottles are placed with it; the
olive-coloured, lead-glazed earthenware
with a cord handle, reminiscent of a
pilgrim's bottle, is particularly splendid.
A silver tea-caddy and a little cup, decorated with Chinese plant arabesques, are
placed on the uncovered table edge in
the interests of a balanced colour scheme.
Despite its painterly refinement the
picture has a certain graphic hardness, as
can also be seen in works by Georges de
La Tour. Stoskopff was a crucial figure in
the development of still-life painting in
Paris from 1620 onwards.   *RM*

Georges de la Tour   (1593–1652)

257   Peasant Couple Eating,
c. 1622/25
Canvas, 76.2 x 90.8 cm
Acquired 1976

The two half-length figures, almost life-
size and tightly framed in the pictorial
space, face the viewer as though they
were caught pausing in their scant meal
of dried peas. The embittered old man
is staring down at the ground in front
of him, while the woman stares at us
fixedly from her deep-set, almost dead
eyes as she raises the spoon to her mouth.
The tanned, furrowed faces and hands
are thrown into sharp and unsparingly
naturalistic relief by the side lighting.
The grey background, which makes it
unclear where this event is taking place,
enhances the presence of the two old
people. It derives from the tradition of
Caravaggio's half-length figures, which
could have been passed on to La Tour by
Hendrick Terbrugghen or Gerard Seghers. Although this picture dates from the
beginning of La Tour's career, c. 1620, it
clearly enjoyed immediate popularity.
there are three 17th-century copies. The
theme of beggars or beggar-musicians
originated in the Netherlands in the
16th century, and could be found in
engravings (e.g. Jacques Callot) in Lorraine, La Tour's homeland in the early
17th century. La Tour was very famous in
his lifetime, but was forgotten soon after
his death. He was not rediscovered until
the first half of the 20th century.   *SM*

Nicolas Poussin (1594–1665)

258 Landscape with Matthew the
Evangelist, 1639/40
Canvas, 99 x 135 cm
Acquired 1873

The French artist Nicolas Poussin is
considered to be the most important
exponent of the classical tendency in
Roman Baroque painting and to have
brought it to perfection. He went to
Rome at the age of thirty and spent the
rest of his life there, with the exception
of a short stay in Paris in 1640/42. He
received commissions from the most
important collectors and patrons in the
papal court circle. The *Landscape with
Matthew the Evangelist* was painted in
1640, for the papal secretary Gian Maria
Roscioli, along with a companion piece,
*Landscape with John the Evangelist on
Patmos* (now in Chicago). It is very
probable that a series of the four Evangelists was originally planned, but that
only two were painted. St. Matthew is
sitting among massive architectural fragments by the riverbank. Behind him is
a spacious landscape with a high, hill-
bound horizon. At John's side is an angel,
the symbol of the Evangelist, inspiring
him to write the Gospel. The principal
theme of this picture is the solemn,

peaceful landscape, similar in some ways
to the Tiber valley north of Rome. The
ruins towering up on the horizon—presumably representing the "Mura di Santo
Stefano" near Anguillara—emphasise the
position of the figures by being placed
directly above them. The figure's concentrated colour-tones of blue, yellow-
orange and white are repeated and
softened in the landscape.   *SM*

Nicolas Poussin (1594–1665)

259 Self-Portrait, 1649
Canvas, 78.7 x 64.8 cm
Acquired 1821

The portrait, defined by muted local
colouring, is placed in front of a relief,
without any particular sense of depth.
The relief shows putti as carriers of laurel
festoons, which are possibly to be seen as
allegorical representations of the children
of night—Death and Sleep? The composition is imbued with an enigmatic
melancholy and is reminiscent of an
epitaph. The self-portrait was intended
for Poussin's Paris friend Paul Fréart de
Chantelou, but the painter seemed to be
dissatisfied with the first (Berlin) Version.
A second version was completed in 1650
and is now in the Louvre. Poussin had

Gaspard Dughet (1615–1675)

260 Roman Mountain Landscape
Canvas, 98.5 x 135.9 cm
Acquired 1904

The landscape painter Gaspard Dughet was born in Rome in 1615 to a French father and an Italian mother. He became a pupil of Poussin, who had married Gaspard's sister the year before, in 1631. He later called himself Gaspard Poussin, after his teacher and brother-in-law. Dughet painted mainly imaginary landscapes based on the Roman *campagna*, whose atmosphere and light he was able to capture like no-one else. With a few exceptions his pictures do not depict identifiable places, but like the Roman *Mountain Landscape*, are invented landscapes. In the distance, beyond a narrow gorge with a waterfall, a sun-soaked hill topped by a little town rises out of the Campagna, which leads out to the horizon with its distant hills. On this side of the gorge, tall trees on the right and left frame a path leading into the distance, with some shepherds on it. Not all of Dughet's pictures are dated; but our picture is dated to 1658/59 by the most recent critical style research.   *SM*

reworked the first version in the meantime, and was thus quite happy to hand it over to the Paris banker and silk manufacturer Jean Pointel.   *RM*

Claude Lorrain (1600–1682)

261 Italian Coastal Landscape in
Morning Light, 1642
Canvas, 97 x 131 cm
Acquired 1881

Claude Gellée, called Claude Lorrain,
was the third great French 17th-century
painter, along with Poussin and his
brother-in-law Gaspard Dughet. Claude
spent almost all his life in Rome, where
he died. He brought classical landscape
art, as developed early in the century
by Paul Bril, Adam Elsheimer, Annibale
Carracci (cf. no. 231), Domenichino
and Agostino Tassi, to one of its high
points. The grand effect of his pictures is
above all due to his use of light, which
comes from the distant horizon and fills
the pictorial space. To a certain extent
Claude's pictures are the opposite extreme to the firmly established tectonics
of Poussin's and Dughet's landscapes (cf.
nos. 258 and 260), even though there
are artistic elements in common. Or-
phaned at the age of twelve, Claude left
his home in Lorraine for Rome, where
he first worked in Agostino Tassi's studio.
After spending two years in Naples he
went back to Lorraine for a short time,
and then finally settled in Rome in the

following year. From then on he painted
for the nobility, high-placed collectors
in Italy and France, cardinals and the
Pope. From about 1635 Claude started
to record his compositions in an album
of drawings, the Liber Veritatis, which is
now in the British Museum in London.
Our picture, dated 1642, is entered in
the Liber Veritatis as number 64, "quadro
faict pour paris. Claudio Gil … inv./R.".
A shepherd is playing a shawm in the
foreground and a woman, reclining on
the rocks, is listening. A path leads into
the distance over a bridge on the left
to the ruins of an ancient temple and a
settlement. On the right the view opens
up over a broad bay, shimmering in the
hazy morning light, and a harbour with
numerous ships in it. To the right of the
shepherd, for no apparent purpose, is a
staff. In fact it is left over from the first
version of the two figures, which was
then painted over. This can now be
seen only on X-ray images, but it is
recorded in Claude's Liber Veritatis. The
staff re-appeared when the picture was
cleaned. *SM*

Diego Velázquez   (1599–1660)

262   Portrait of a Lady
Canvas, 123.7 x 101.7 cm
Acquired 1887

If Zurbarán, Velázquez's contemporary and fellow Andalusian, remained committed throughout his life to stark contrasts of light and shade, Velázquez did not. After he moved to court his own handling of light began to look very modern; it became increasingly sophisticated and yet realistic, incomparably so for his times. He mastered the art of conveying atmospheric values subtly. The effect of this portrait of a lady derives not least from the neutral, light-grey ground, and the subject's face and hair, which are blurred when we examine them closely but from a distance seem to be seen through the dust-filled air of an inner chamber. The chair, a stylistic device that Velázquez used frequently is an example of Velázquez's ability to derive the strongest effects from restricted resources: as the sole prop, it seems to have appeared in the room by chance, but it allows the lady to achieve a stately pose. A note on the back of the picture led to the earlier belief that she was the painter's wife, but she is now usually thought to be Countess Monterrey, the wife of a Spanish ambassador and sister of Livares. She lived in Italy, which indicates that the picture was painted as early as 1631, when Velázquez first returned from Rome.   *MW*

him up as if he were on a stage. The hint of a step, the sharply defined shadow cast by the subject and the sophisticated lighting at the same time secure the Berlin picture a sense of spaciousness which we do not find in the artist's earlier works. As in his saints, which often seem wooden, the spectacular handling of light and colour conceal weaknesses in the drawing. *MW*

Bartolomé Esteban Murillo
(1618–1682)

264   The Baptism of Christ, c. 1655
Canvas, 233.2 x 160.1 cm
Acquired 1968

The John the Baptist series was probably painted c. 1655 for the monastery of San Leandro in Murillo's home town of Seville (where it remained until 1812), and it marks an important step in the development of Murillo's mature style. *The Baptism of Christ* already demonstrates mastery of brushwork, reticent colouring and delicately blurred faces, but the forms are not yet so delicately linked together, and the astringent, profoundly serious atmosphere has none of the sweetness of many of his later works,

Francisco de Zurbarán
(1598–1664)

263   Don Alonso Verdugo de Albornoz
1635 or 1636
Canvas, 186.6 x 104.5 cm
Acquired 1906

This picture is a highly valued piece in the small Spanish collection in Berlin, for there exist no other signed portraits and no other secular portraits of this calibre by Zurbarán (in 1945 a large work by Zurbarán was stolen from the collection).

The coat of arms in the top right-hand corner is that of the Andalusian nobleman Don Alonso Verdugo de Albornoz. He is wearing the green cross of the Order of the Knights of Alcántara on his chest. The baton, sash, and the inclusion of his age in the bottom right-hand corner of the picture can be explained by the fact that he took over the mounted bodyguard of his uncle, who was an important personality at court. As in the case of dozens of similarly conceived saints, Zurbarán chisels him, sharply lit, out of the neutral ground, which sets

of which the Berlin gallery owned two significant examples until 1945. Murillo clearly surpasses an altar-panel painted by Rubens in Mechelen, which is known to us from drawings and to which Murillo's composition owes a great deal, particularly in the naturalness of the pictorial structure with the two life-size figures. A sprinkling of written quotations emphasises the didactic quality of the picture, which was reduced in height and breadth by about 20 centimetres, which rendered incomplete the proclamation of God the Father. After the reduction the artist's signature was placed somewhat higher.   *MW*

Jean Antoine Watteau
(1684–1721)

265   The Dance (Iris), 1717/19
Canvas, 97.5 x 166 cm
Loan from the German Federal Republic

This painting, presumably originally horizontally oval, derived its ambiguous title from a quatrain added to Charles-Nicolas Cochin's reversed reproduction engraving dated c. 1726 (?). The monumental figure of a girl is placed in front of a low horizon. Elegantly dressed shepherd boys, one of them even playing a musical instrument, are eagerly waiting for the dreamy coquette's dance to begin. The neutrality of the theme is further supported by props depicted in the left, the "valiant" shield with arrow, which are to be read as anticipating the deployment of feminine charms. The dress is made of typical 1718 English printed silks. Watteau presumably painted the picture during his only trip abroad, to England in 1719/20. Like almost all his works, this one, carried by its muted colours, is essentially ornamental. The painting was purchased by Frederick the Great before 1769, and was found in the estate of his brother, Prince Heinrich, in Schloss Rheinsberg, in 1802.   *RM*

Jean Antoine Watteau
(1684–1721)

266 The French Comedy; The Italian
Comedy, c. 1715/17
Canvas, 37.5 x 49 cm/38.3 x 48.7 cm
Acquired from the Royal Palaces, 1829

The painter was a member of the
Academy from 30 July, 1712. When
registering his diploma piece in 1717:
The Embarkation for the Island of Cythera
(Paris, Louvre), the title was corrected
to "une fête galante". The Academicians
were thus defining a genre for the first
time which was in the future to remain
inseparably linked with the painter's
name. The two Berlin counterparts have
been passed down by the reproduction
engravings of Charles-Nicolas Cochin
confirming the titles from 1734, and
have been linked from time immemorial.
Their ultimately obscure iconography
and similar formats always caused them
to be seen together and in comparison.

The French Comedy (above) focuses on
a group gathered in front of altar-like architecture in a park: Bacchus is drinking
to a noble huntsman (Cupid). The bond
between them is concluded by Columbine, the female personification of foolish love (*la folie*). A couple is hesitantly
starting to dance in front of this allegory.
Near the top of the painting is a bust on
a pillar—Momus—son of the night and
personification of foolish addiction to
criticism.

In *The Italian Comedy* (opposite page,
top), Watteau's only night-piece, the
performers seem to be acknowledging
the audience's applause at the end of a
performance. The picture is dominated
by Pierrot with his guitar and Mezzetino
with the torch. On the left is Columbine
with a mask in her hand, and Isabella
turning to Pantalone. On the right we
can see Doctor Marcisino leaning on a
stick and Scaramuccia. Watteau's pictures,
placed in the narrow realm between illusion and reality in terms of their subject
matter, present us with a number of pictorial riddles. The two Berlin pictures are
among his most famous works and were
acquired by Frederick the Great before
1766 for the picture gallery in the park
of Sanssouci, built to a plan by Büring in
1764.   *RM*

Jean Baptiste Siméon Chardin
(1699–1779)

267 The Draughtsman, 1737
Canvas, 81.3 x 65 cm
Acquired 1931

A boy concentrating on everyday prose dominates the composition. He is sharpening his chalk with apparent care, partly covering the light-blue paper with his arm. Pastel shades, unspectacular in their varied intensity, indicate depth. Various objects are introduced into the picture but with appropriate economy. The image approaches an almost emblematic codification of striving artistry. It is said that the youth, Auguste-Gabriel Godefroy, a goldsmith's son, was a frequent guest in the painter's studio.

Chardin, who never left his home town of Paris, painted mainly from nature; as far as we know he did not use preliminary drawings. This method, which was unheard-of at the time, as well as the models he used, caring motherly figures, virtuous cooks and nicely-behaved children, were much admired by the new bourgeois art criticism as practised by Diderot, constituting a moral counterpart to Boucher's frivolous pictorial world. The Berlin painting is presumed to have been acquired by Frederick the Great in 1747.   *RM*

Jean François de Troy
(1679–1752)

268 Bacchus and Ariadne, 1717
Canvas, 140 x 165 cm
Acquired 1961. Property of the
Kaiser Friedrich-Museums-Verein

The god of wine is consoling the
abandoned daughter of the Cretan king
Minos. She has been left on the island
of Naxos by the Athenian Theseus, who
can be seen sailing away in the distance,
after she had helped him destroy the bull
who was tyrannising their homeland.
Ovid's *Metamorphoses* (VIII, 310–317)
give an account including a red thread
that helped the hero find his way out of
the notorious labyrinth. Hymen, the god
of marriage, is hovering auspiciously over
the two main protagonists. The exuber-
ant retinue of maenads and goat-like
satyrs, and even the drunken Silenus,
Bacchus's former tutor, on the left on
an ass, to a certain extent transform
Ariadne's pain into a happy event. History painter de Troy returns here to the
heroic landscapes of Claude Lorrain and
Nicolas Poussin, while also moving towards the more modern Rococo painting style shown in his lighter accents for
the figures. Along with its counterpart,
The Education of Bacchus (1717), it is

exhibited in the Bode-Museum (upper
floor, room 257).   RM

Jean Restout   (1692–1768)

269   The Magnanimity of Scipio,
1728
Canvas, 132 x 196.8 cm
Acquired 1983

This painting is in the tradition of pictorial reflection on legendary heroic
historiography, but nevertheless the artist
gave the theme something of the character of a morality painting. The Roman
conqueror of New Carthage (on the
Iberian peninsula), identified by a plinth
as well as a red cloak, is demonstratively
renouncing his booty, the bride of the
Celtiberian Allucius, who has fallen on
his knees and embraced Scipio's arm in
gratitude. The magnificent Baroque still
life that the parents are offering Scipio
in exchange for their daughter did not
affect his generous decision, as he left
everything for the couple as a wedding
present. Here it serves to decorate the
scene, like the attendants and repoussoir
figures. Restout chose the subject from
Livy's Roman history and transformed
it into a moving sentimental piece. The
choice of colour, which is lighter than in

late 17th-century French painting, and the use of contemporary (theatrical) costume, was presumably intended to bring the message of the painting, namely that moderation should be cultivated, lastingly up to date. *RM*

court sculptor Frémin (1672–1744) also worked for the Spanish court on the Iberian peninsula.

The colours and composition of the painting offer a typical example of art at the end of the age of Louis XIV. *RM*

Nicolas de Largillierre
(1656–1746)

270 The Sculptor René Frémin in his Studio, c. 1713
Canvas, 135.5 x 109.2 cm
Acquired 1980

This is a celebration of the Baroque topos of artistic genius. The sculptor moves with consummate ease between raw, unformed material in the foreground and a completed work in the background, in the form of the *Belvedere Torso*. The strict canon of the times required programmatic orientation towards Hellenistic art and art of the imperial Roman period, and their preservation in contemporary artefacts. The creative process for *Zephyr and Flora*, a group of figures that Frémin made in 1713, operates in terms of this ideal. This sculpture, planned for the Trianon Palace in the park of Versailles, was probably never carried out. The highly regarded French

François Boucher (1703–1770)

271 Venus and Cupid, 1742
Canvas, 58.6 x 73.7 cm
Acquired 1978. Property of the
Kaiser Friedrich-Museums-Verein

Anadyomene (she who is born of the
foam) is resting in a secluded landscape,
lowering her eyes in shame while at the
same time flaunting her nakedness. She is
appropriately painted in subdued colours.
This background seems to be prompted
by the boscages—artificial groups of
small woods—that were so popular at
the time. The great shell of the cascade
that feeds the stream in the foreground
indicates the goddess's origins. She is co-
quettishly dipping her foot into it while
her son seems to be teasing cooing doves.
The Berlin composition is clear evidence
of Boucher's high art of ornamentation,
which dominated his brilliant tapestry
designs for the factory in Beauvais. The
painter transformed Watteau's profound
pastorales into popular social pieces, fun-
damentally driven by the artistic culture
of Rococo in their decorative dominance. The small format and the intimacy
of the presentation support the assumption that the Berlin painting adorned an
area that was largely not accessible to the
public. "Only when Venus sleeps is the
world at peace." This apt creed is taken
from a sextet found under an 18th-cen-
tury reproduction engraving.   *RM*

Hubert Robert (1733–1808)

272 The Ruins of Nîmes, Orange and
Saint-Rémy-de-Provence
c. 1783/1789
Canvas, 117 x 174 cm
Acquired 1936

As a student at the French Academy
of Arts in Rome, Robert was lastingly
affected by the work of Panini and Pira-
nesi. In the period from 1785 to 1787 he
composed pictures of ruins in Provence,
and the Berlin painting is possibly one
of these. It reflects the most significant
remains of ancient Roman architecture
north of the Alps. Nîmes in the south of
France was called Nemausus in Roman
times. From left to right it is possible to
identify the ruins of the amphitheatre, of
a pseudodipteral temple (Maison Car-
reé), of the aqueduct (Pont du Gard), the
mausoleum of Saint Rémy, the Julian
Arch and the theatre of Orange. Robert

handled real things consummately. For him, architecture was the starting-point for original artistic ideas. In this respect he moved away from accepted *veduta* painting. It is therefore not an anachronism when figures in ancient costume populate the ruined site of their former civilisation. Elements of paraphrased but precise architectural drawing and a warm sense of colour determine the enigmatic, indeed philosophical dimension of this painting. *RM*

times, using graphically rigorous drawing and precise local colour. The painting's tendentious, though intimate character, in other words the exact artistic reproduction of an immaculate body makes it significantly more difficult to respond to the work. *RM*

Elisabeth Louise Vigée-Lebrun
(1755–1842)

273   Prince Heinrich Lubomirski as the Genius of Fame, 1789
Canvas, 105.5 x 83 cm
Acquired 1974

The androgynous child with white wings is holding up a garland of myrtle and laurel as a symbol of innocence triumphant. But his "day-dreaming" facial expression immediately puts the interpretation back in question, as there is an auspicious quiver full of arrows at his side. Thus he could potentially also be seen as a trouble-making Cupid. The image of the prince was created according to the classical artistic theory of the

Sir Joshua Reynolds
(1723–1792)

274 Lord Robert Clive and his Family
with an Indian Servant Girl, c.1765/1766
Canvas, 140.8 x 173.7 cm
Acquired 1978

Clive, a priest's son, was a combatant on
behalf of the British Crown in India.
He returned to his homeland a wealthy
man. In 1763 he became engaged to
Sidney Bolton, who is depicted here.
The eldest daughter was born in 1764
and died at an early age; she was to have
formed the centrepiece of the right-hand
group. Mother and servant are carefully
supporting the child, who is dressed in
costly Indian silk. The left-hand third of
the picture was added a little later, painting over the landscape behind the servant
girl. Possibly this change was brought
about by the death of the child, because
now the family seems to be united as in
an epitaph. This has made the composition unconcentrated, indeed even disor-
ganised. However, Reynolds still reveals
his debt to 17th-century Flemish painting, a tradition that had been carried on
in England by Kneller and Lely. He pre-

sented costly fabrics with great virtuosity,
using refined highlighting achieved by
white enhancements. At the same time
the master and his studio successfully
introduced an austere type of dignity
into the portraits by comparatively hard
treatment of line.   RM

Sir Joshua Reynolds
(1723–1792)

275 Lady Sunderland, 1786
Canvas, 238.5 x 147.5 cm
Acquired 1983

The woman depicted is the eldest
daughter of Godolphin Rooper. In 1778
she married a rich London barrister,
whom King George III created Baron
Sunderland of Lake in 1785. A rich
silk robe and chiffon shawl interwoven
with gold hide the flesh-tints, which are
executed in cold shades. Just as in the
17th-century Flemish painting that was
so universally popular in England at the
time, the sculpturally rendered figure
is placed in front of a section of ideal
landscape. This background, which is to
an extent developed from the colour,

and forms create an agreeable contrast with the graphic hardness of the figure. Reynolds, who was President of the Royal Academy, provides a striking example of 18th-century English classicism with this late work. Baron Sunderland paid his fee for this work in November 1786. This fact confirms the dating of the Berlin painting. *RM*

Sir Thomas Lawrence
(1769–1830)

276 The Angerstein Children, 1807
Canvas, 184.3 x 148.8 cm
Acquired 1979

Lawrence came to London as an unknown pastel painter in 1787. His fame as an artist soon spread. His clients included the court and influential families. The painter started to work for Julius Angerstein, a banker and collector of old painting, on this group portrait of his grandchildren at his country home, Woodlands, on 17 August, 1807. The Angerstein collection was later purchased by the English government from the estate. These paintings helped to form the initial collection of the National Gallery in London, which was founded in 1824.

For the group portrait of the Angerstein children, Lawrence used subdued colours that gave an impression of scraps of colour through pronounced white highlights. The red curtain, in fact entirely inappropriate in a park, frames the dark landscape background in a most picturesque fashion. Two of the children, Elizabeth Julia and John Julius, are posted at the front extremities of the picture like Baroque *repoussoir* figures. The boy with the besom is reminiscent of images of George the dragon-slayer. Henry Frederick and Caroline Amelia occupy the centre of the picture.

The painting has a subliminally theatrical quality, suggesting a contemporary preference for historical stylistic forms even in the early years of the century. Lawrence had already exhibited a group

portrait (in the Louvre) of the Angerstein children in the Royal Academy in London in 1800. However, this is dominated by a sense of formality and prestige, further heightened by a large column, the traditional symbol of dignity. *RM*

is alleged that she was the daughter of a duke. She used this fact to justify her magnificent toilet. Gainsborough integrated the model into the landscape in a way that is typical of him. This meant that the surroundings could be used as a psychological "sounding board". The Berlin picture is marked by enormous painterly brilliance, and was probably painted in Bath, the fashionable English spa where Gainsborough lived until 1760. He was the most important English 18th-century painter after Reynolds.   *RM*

Thomas Gainsborough
(1727–1788)

277   Portrait of Margaret Burr
c. 1758
Canvas, 76 x 63.5 cm
Acquired 1958

In 1747, at the age of only about 19, the subject of the portrait married the painter. Mrs Gainsborough was considered to be very pretty, pleasant and virtuous. It

Thomas Gainsborough
(1727–1788)

278   John Wilkinson
c. 1775
Canvas, 234 x 145 cm
Acquired 1904

From about 1770 the subject's company supplied cast parts for England's first iron bridge. From July 1779 it crossed the river Severn in the English Midlands between Madeley and Broseley with a span of about 32 metres, not far from Ironbridge, which of course took its name from this wonder of the Industrial Revolution. Gainsborough integrated his subject into the landscape in typical fashion. Wilkinson sits in his casually painted natural surroundings as calmly as a country gentleman. The modelling of the figure can still be made out in some phases of the work. There is a lack of strict linear detail in the drapery. This means that the picture as a whole makes an astonishingly lively impression. Where traditional portrait painters and their successors made use of an enormous repertoire of draperies, architectural detail and furniture, Gainsborough used depictions of living plants. The picture was probably painted in Gainsborough's studio, Schomberg House in Pall Mall. This was one of the first products of the English School to arrive in the Gemäldegalerie collection.   *RM*

Thomas Gainsborough
(1727–1788)

279 The Marsham Children, 1787
Canvas, 242.9 x 181.9 cm
Acquired 1982

Charles Marsham, 1st Earl of Romney, commissioned a life-size group portrait of his children Amelia Charlotte, Frances, Harriot and Charles from the much sought-after Gainsborough in July 1787. The children are surrounded by an impressive late summer landscape created entirely from colour. For all the picture's ostentatious informality, the children relate to each other only formally as they collect hazelnuts. Their eyes meet only with difficulty, so that the composition is lacking in convincing inner rapport. It is clear that Gainsborough added the faces after separate portrait sittings. The apparently spontaneous manner of painting is the product of carefully considered studio planning. This means that the usual distance involved in official portraits in removed in Gainsborough's magnificent late work, but the sense of dignity remains.   *RM*

John Hoppner (1758–1810)

280 Portrait of John Jeffreys Pratt, 2nd Earl and 1st Marquess of Camden, as a Knight of the Order of the Garter, 1806
Canvas, 249.2 x 158.3 cm
Acquired 1981

George III created Pratt a Knight of the Garter in 1799, and the Governor of Ireland is wearing the vestments of that order here. The velvet band from which

the name derives can be seen below his left knee, with the motto "Honi soit qui mal y pense". A miniature portrait of St. George, the patron saint of the Order, hangs on the magnificent chain. Hoppner was a master of the traditional repertoire of Flemish Baroque painting: massive columns, a heavy velvet curtain and "heroic" clouds in the background. The artist flattered his clients with a lavish display of colour, and thus advanced to be London society's favourite portrait painter, alongside Thomas Lawrence. The Berlin picture appeared in the 1806 Royal Academy exhibition (no. 77). RM

Richard Wilson, attributed to (1714–1782)

281 Landscape with River Valley
Oil on canvas, 133 x 209 cm
Acquired 1905

Wilson was a friend of Reynolds, and was a member of the Royal Academy from 1769. This composition in subdued colours is intensified by the river valley. It leads into the staggered depths of the landscape, which seems almost to dissolve in the background. The figures and the bizarre trees on the right form a well-conceived frame for this idealistic back-drop. It seems to be inspired by the

heroic landscapes of Claude Lorrain and Salvator Rosa in its glowing colour and ideas. *RM*

Sir Henry Raeburn   (1756–1823)

282   Sir James Montgomery,
Bart. 1801
Canvas, 225 x 148 cm
Acquired 1908

Raeburn was a protégé of Reynolds. He returned to his Scottish home after spending two years in Italy. He became Edinburgh's leading portrait painter. In 1822, George IV made him the King's Limner for Scotland.

The subject was a successful land-owner and lawyer who worked as Lord Advocate in Edinburgh from 1766. He is shown here in his function as Lord Chief of the Scottish Exchequer, hence the chequered tablecloth, the books with bookmarks at the front, the bundles of documents and the large royal seal. With great dignity, in his robes of office he confronts the column which from time immemorial has symbolised the quality of endurance. The painting's rich colours owe much to 17th-century Flemish por-traiture, which considerably influenced British painting. *RM*

picture was confirmed as depicting a bacchante.

The work hung opposite is its counterpart, a picture of Ceres (in private ownership). Later, (1793) the "Bacchante" arrived in the Berlin Royal Palace, the residence of King Friedrich Wilhelm II of Prussia, as an "Ariadne". *RM*

Maria Angelica Kauffmann
(1741–1807)

283   Bacchante
before May 1785
Canvas, 76.7 x 64.2 cm
Acquired from the Royal Palaces, 1829

This stylised portrait favours delicate colouring and the decorative presence of Rococo. The artist lived in England from 1766 to 1781, and it is probable that *Bacchante* was painted sometime during these years. When Kauffmann moved to Rome in 1872, she took this painting with her. In Rome, it was acquired in 1785 by Duke Peter Biron of Courland for his palace in Friedrichsfelde near Berlin. It was also there in 1786 that the

Antoine Pesne (1683–1757)

284 Self-Portrait with his Daughters
Henriette Joyard and Marie de Rège at
the easel, 1754
Canvas, 179.4 x 151.2 cm
Acquired 1903

The Prussian court painter depicted
himself here at a moment of apparently
uninterrupted activity. The group of
figures is placed in a calculated triangle,
which balances the composition. The
fact that the three people are so close
together is intended to indicate the
intimacy of their relationship.

The daughters are sharing their
father's activity, like muses providing
inspiration. Two books are casually placed
on the right-hand edge of the picture,

one of which is Ovid's *Metamorphoses*.
The painter often used this amorous
literature as a thematic programme.
The volume is lying on a piece of light
blue paper showing Venus and Cupid.
Next to this is a cast head of a statue of
Apollo, the leader of the Muses.

Warm colours are juxtaposed with
occasional pastel shades. This sort of
colouring was a key feature of Pesne's
paintings, which were a major influence
on Rococo painting at the time of
Frederick the Great. This self-portrait
was presumably painted in Pesne's studio
on Friedrichswerder in Berlin.   *RM*

Antoine Pesne (1683–1757)

285   Portrait of Frederick the Great as
Crown Prince, 1739/40
Canvas, 80.5 x 65 cm
Acquired 1841

We owe this famous portrait to the
painter's friendship with the heir to the
Prussian throne. It shows Frederick in a
black cuirass with the orange sash of the
Order of the Black Eagle over it, and also
the magnificent ermine-trimmed coronation robe, fastened with a diamond
brooch. Under this the Crown Prince is
wearing a picturesque paraphrase of the
uniform of his 1st bodyguard battalion,
infantry regiment no. 15-I, which was
stationed in Neuruppin. This was to be
the last authentic portrait of Frederick
until 1763. It was reproduced with minor
changes by Georg Friedrich Schmidt,
who was the Prussian court copperplate
engraver and a friend of Pesnes, in 1746.
The painting was frequently copied with
a number of variations in the painter's
studio and other places. In creating it
Pesne had established a standard form
for presenting a ruler, even while at the
Crown Prince's court in Rheinsberg.
The portrait is a major achievement
of Rococo in the age of Frederick the
Great.   *RM*

prefer the art of Maria Angelica Kauffmann. Von Maron turns to us out of
the picture with a calm and thoughtful
expression. He is clutching a number of
paintbrushes to his chest in an unpreten-
tious fashion. Here the Baroque pose is
abandoned in favour of a psychological
approach, which brings the work close to
the portraits of Anton Graff. Von Maron's
paintings combine Neo-Classical formal
austerity with a sophisticated sense of
colour.   *RM*

Anton von Maron
(1731–1808)

286   Self-Portrait, 1794
Canvas, 73 x 60 cm
Acquired 1952

Von Maron was born in Vienna, but
lived in Rome from 1756, where he
continued to train under Anton Raphael
Mengs. In 1776 he reformed the Vien-
nese Academy of Art, presumably the
reason for his being raised to the peerage
by Empress Maria Theresa. The Berlin
picture dates from a period when the
painter was becoming increasingly iso-
lated. His works were much in demand
until the early 1790s, but then the public
in his adoptive Roman home began to

Johann Heinrich Tischbein the Elder (1722–1789)

287 Portrait of Prince Heinrich of Prussia, 1769
Canvas, 147.5 x 113 cm
Acquired 1955. Property of the
Kaiser Friedrich-Museums-Verein

This is a commemorative portrait for the Battle of Freiberg in Saxony on 29 October, 1762. The pantherskin cuffs and lapels on the uniform coat, the silver general's armband, the band and star of the Prussian Order of the Black Eagle,

and on it the cross of a canon of Magdeburg cathedral, emphasise the prince's prominent social position. *RM*

Anna Dorothea Therbusch, née Liszewska (1721–1782)

288 Self-Portrait (Unfinished)
1776/77
Canvas, 153.5 x 118 cm
Acquired 1924

This Berlin painter was a member of several artistic academies (Stuttgart, Paris, Vienna). She maintained a studio on the prestigious Unter den Linden boulevard in Berlin from 1773. This self-portrait is a mature work, and shows Therbusch as a Vestal Virgin beside a tripod topped with fire. The austere life of a priestess of the Roman goddess of the domestic hearth seems to be a metaphor of her own arduous existence as a woman painter. Her expression, as she looks up from her book, is reminiscent of that of a Sybil. The subject gazes forcefully at the viewer through her imposing eyeglass. The red paint she used as an undercoat for her portraits can still be made out. *RM*

Johann Heinrich Tischbein the Elder (1722–1789)

289 Self-Portrait with his First Wife at the Clavichord, 1756/57
Canvas, 51 x 39.5 cm
Acquired 1913

Tischbein was appointed court painter to Landgrave Wilhelm VIII of Hesse-Kassel from 1753, and lived in Kassel from 1754. He married Marie Sophie Robert in 1756. The Berlin picture must have been painted shortly after that. The artist breaks off from his work to follow his wife's keen interest in music. The presentation of the married couple is carefully balanced as a result of both the composition and the subdued intensity of the colours. In the background is a primed canvas with the underpainting for figures.

Tischbein completed this painting in 1757. It shows Menelaus in combat with Paris, who is rescued by Venus (Schloss Wilhelmshöhe, Kassel). The fact that the initial stages of the assisting goddess can be made out can be interpreted as an allusion to the marital happiness portrayed. There is no definite answer to the question of the extent to which the picture reproduces emblematic notions from earlier centuries, i.e. is indicating the harmony between the sister arts of painting and music. But it is more probable that it shows the unsophisticated delight in storytelling of a citizen of Hesse who has acquired a certain prosperity.   *RM*

Georg David Matthieu
(1737–1778)

290   Portraits of Kammerrat Joachim Ulrich von Giese and His Wife Sophie Elisabeth, née von Schwerin, 1762/64
Canvas, each 142 x 106 cm
Acquired 1928

Matthieu was appointed court painter to Duke Friedrich of Mecklenburg-Schwerin in Ludwigslust in 1764, and his portraits show consummate mastery of the Baroque art repertoire. He arranged costly furniture and clothes, with a view from below in a sophisticated fashion.

Giese founded an important faience factory in Stralsund in 1755. Here he is shown as a passionate music-lover rather than a successful businessman. Matthieu must have painted this pair of portraits during his stay in Stralsund. It is possible that they were intended for Giese's country house in Niederhof, West Pomerania. The possibility that the painting shows interior details of this building, which was destroyed in 1947, cannot be ruled out.   *RM*

Christian Bernhardt Rode
(1725–1797)

291 Frederick the Great at the Camp-Fire before the Battle of Torgau, 1791
Canvas, 118 x 151 cm
Acquired 1923

An anecdote relates that the king leant thoughtfully against an oak. He is watching over the sleep of his faithful servant, the Hussar General Zieten. A soldier's wife is placing a pot of potatoes on the provisional hearth, without noticing the gentlemen. She is fanning the ashes so enthusiastically that ash is being blown in the king's face. However, he graciously allows her to continue, while he protects himself with his cloak. The glow of the camp-fire highlights the protagonists.

The painting was shown at the 1793 Berlin Academy exhibition (picture no. 2). It was part of a loosely compiled Brandenburgiana (Fridericiana) that came into being between 1787 or 1791 and 1795.   *RM*

Daniel Nikolaus Chodowiecki
(1726–1801)

292 Jean Calas Bids his Family Farewell before the Execution on March 10, 1762; 1765/66
Canvas, 30.7 x 42.5 cm
Acquired 1865

Jean Calas, a Calvinist merchant from Toulouse, was executed on the basis of slanderous accusations. A horrified Chodowiecki discovered that this terrible event had taken place in the same year, from a French copperplate engraving. After copying this picture in oil he decided to paint the companion-piece that we see here. Chodowiecki responded to the great public interest in the picture by offering etchings (1767/68), which reproduced the painting in the same format. This picture enabled him to make a break-through as a successful illustrator.   *RM*

Hans Bol (1534–1593)

293 The Fishermen's Battle, 1585
Watercolour on parchment, 11 x 17 cm
Acquired 1830

In this miniature the artist shows a popular sporting competition on a small lake in The Hague, in which the competitors try to push each other into the water with wooden poles. Bol's drawn and engraved landscapes made him one of the main exponents of this branch of Dutch art in the 16th century, along with Hieronymus Cock and Pieter Bruegel the Elder. These gouache paintings are a genre in their own right, known as cabinet pictures; they were highly sought-after by princely collectors. *RC*

Alexander Cooper
(c. 1605–1660)

294 Chain of Medallions with Portraits of Friedrich V of the Palatinate, his Wife and Children, 1632/33
Gouache on parchment, each 3 x 2.6 cm, mounts: gold and enamel
Acquired 1902

In 1613 the "Winter King", Frederick V, became engaged to Elizabeth Stuart of England. The portraits of the royal couple suggest stylistic influence by Hoskins the Elder or van Dyck. Cooper presumably came from London, and worked in The Hague from 1631, where the Berlin medallion chain was probably also produced. *RM*

Godfried Schalcken   (1634–1706)

295   Self-Portrait with Burning
Candle (Oval)
Oil on paper, oak, 10.3 x 8.2 cm
Acquired 1894

Schalcken, sometimes called the "master
of light", liked to depict a light-source,
preferably a burning candle, in portraits
or landscapes so as to produce a delicately sculptural, three-dimensional quality.
The succinct characterisation of the face
and the intimately diffuse atmosphere
of the surroundings give the miniature
format a particular intensity. When we
compare this with positively identified self-portraits, for example the 1695
portrait in Florence (Uffizi) or the one
painted in England (Leamington Spa), it

is clear that the signed Berlin picture is
of the artist himself. The blonde wig
suggests that it was painted later.
Schalcken trained first under Samuel
van Hoogstraten in Dordrecht, then
under Gerard Dou in Leiden. He is
indebted to Dou both for his skill in
fine painting and his preference for small
formats. He was extremely productive
and successful as a portrait-painter to
the nobility in two stays in England,
from 1703 at the court in Düsseldorf
and ultimately also at the court of the
house of Orange in The Hague. His
work was particularly highly esteemed
in the 18th century. Today he is seen as
a typical master of the period of Dutch
decline, with all its virtuoso craftsman-
ship and mannered quality. The oval
Berlin portrait is in a stylistically

remarkable carved frame that could derive from copperplate work by the Augsburg engraver Raphael Custos (1590–1651).

IG

Joseph Werner the Younger
(1637–1710)

296 Flora Crowning a Monkey, 1685
Gouache on parchment over copper,
10 x 8.6 cm
Acquired 1894

Werner appears to have created the gouache because he was depressed by the prosaic mentality of his Bern home. A powerful tree-trunk covered with tendrils, luxuriant tree-tops on the horizon, a lavish bouquet and ripe fruits form a high point of general perfection. The pedestal decorated with a faun carries only empty plinths, and there are small ruins everywhere. Flora, the goddess of spring and blossoms, is reclining in this pictorial scene, warning us that we should be aware of transience. She seems frozen, like a marble sculpture. Only the garland on her head escapes from the mannered chill. Flora, without any apparent interest, is giving another garland to the stupidly staring monkey, a species that had always stood for a vain instinct to imitate, and that symbolises evil. This grotesque coronation must have been read as an allegory of past folly. This miniature was in the Kurbrandenburgische Kunstkammer in the Berlin Stadtschloss as early as 9 December, 1689 (as picture no. 62).

RM

Edict of Nantes in 1685, and returned home to Geneva in 1687. The paint was meticulously dabbed on to the thin (single colour) enamel support before melting, which is one of the main reasons for the brilliant appearance of the king in his cuirass. The portrait could be a reference to the successful "Mars", who was well known to have conquered massive areas of the Empire with his capable generals. The finely chased gold frame with a blue enamelled edge shows that the miniature must have originally been mounted in the top of the lid of a valuable box. This could have been a state gift, of a kind that was very popular at the time.

RM

Jean Petitot (1607–1691)

297 Portrait of Louis XIV of France before 1685
Enamel, 2.6 x 2.5 cm
Acquired 1894

Louis XIV appointed Petitot, the outstanding enamel painter of the time, to be court medal-maker in Versailles in about 1650. The artist was persecuted for his Protestant faith after revocation of the

Daniel Nikolaus Chodowiecki
(1726–1801)

298 Self-Portrait while Drawing with
his Wife Opposite c. 1759
Watercolour on ivory, 8.3 x 10.9 cm
Acquired 1931

On 18 July, 1755, the artist married
Jeanne Barez, the daughter of a French
embroiderer in gold. They moved first of
all into the Rollet house in Brüderstrasse
in Berlin, which belonged to Barez's
relatives. It is possible that the miniature
was created here.

This watercolour on ivory was painted correctly according to instructions
in a contemporary lexicon, "starting by
applying the paint, and the ground
underpainting in large, even strokes, but
not as strongly at first as it is intended to
turn out, as the colour is strengthened
by the dots."

In front of the window on the desk,
an open box used to keep paint pots and
a container with little bottles for painting
materials can be seen. Jeanne Chodowiecki is holding a portrait of her friend
Louise Erman.

The painter used a magnifying glass
in order to finish his portraits with the
maximum refinement and liveliness of
expression. This method led to a considerable success and set the artist apart
from other competitors in this field,
something that did not go unnoticed by
writers, publishers and book dealers, such
as Christoph Friedrich Nicolai in Berlin,
at least with regard to miniaturists working with enamel.

This exquisite ivory miniature still has
its original Rococo frame.   *RM*

C. Vernet
(worked in Königsberg, Prussia after
1790, and in Russia)

299 Portrait of Immanuel Kant c. 1792
Watercolour on paper, 10.6 x 8.2 cm
Acquired 1894

The Prussian philosopher Kant never left
his home town. Vernet (his first name is
not known), a pupil of Therbusch, thus
painted this small, unflattering portrait in
Königsberg. An inscription on the back
revealed that Kant sat for the painter.
Vernet concentrates on the face, largely
neglecting the setting. He "lit" the sharp
features by using white highlights. The
great thinker's look has effectively turned
inwards, which gives the portrait a highly
intimate character. A reproduction engraving of the miniature, itself created by
Vernet in several version, was advertised
in 1797   *RM*

Carl Friedrich Thienpondt
(1730–1796)

300 Self-Portrait, 1761
Enamel, 6.2 x 4.8 cm
Acquired 1920

Here the colours were applied in dots
onto the single-colour pre-enamelled
metal ground, following the approach
that was customary at the time. This
technique makes the portrait look like
a small porcelain image. Fine nuances
are set alongside less saturated contrasting
colours in a masterly fashion. Thienpondt, a pupil of Pesne, was a highly
sought-after miniature painter working in Berlin. Later a pupil of Raphael
Mengs' in Dresden, he spent most of the
Seven Years War (1756–63) in Berlin.

In a letter dated April 1758, Christoph
Friedrich Nicolai wrote: "... it is scarcely
credible how beloved the miniature has
become, especially enamel painting on
boxes or other similar objects. There are
reputed to be some 150 enamel artists
in Berlin; however, apart from five or
six, they are of little significance. I have
forgotten in this respect to mention
the name of Mr. Tienpont, who indeed
understands how to render his works to
great effect."

Thienpondt is understood to have
moved to Warsaw later. Only a very few
of his miniatures are known today.   *RM*

Index of Artists

Numbers in this index refer to entries and not pages